IAN R. MITCHELL was born in Aberdeen, and his formative mountaineering took place on the Upper Deeside march of the Cairngorms in the 1960s. These years, which included a couple of audiences with members of the Royal Family, are described in Ian's classic account of that period, *Mountain Days and Bothy Nights* (co-authored with Dave Brown, and published by Luath Press). Despite moving to Glasgow, Ian has maintained his links with the mountains and bothies of the Braes o Mar, which continue to feature in his works, most recently *Scotland's Mountains before the Mountaineers* – also published by Luath. He is currently completing his second round of the Munros, and his first of the Corbetts, which activities take him back regularly to Deeside.

Ian now writes full-time, supplemented by giving talks and slide shows, and organising historical/cultural tours in the mountains. He is the winner of both the Boardman-Tasker Prize for Mountain Literature for *A View from the Ridge* (also co-authored with Dave Brown), and the Outdoor Writers' Guild Award for Excellence for *Scotland's Mountains before the Mountaineers*. He is currently preparing for publication an historical novel based on the life of Ewan MacPhee, the last mountain bandit. *On the Trail of Queen Victoria in the Highlands* is his eighth book on Scottish mountain themes.

Now available in Luath's *On the Trail of* series

# On the Trail of
# Queen Victoria
# in the Highlands

IAN R. MITCHELL

**Luath** Press Limited

EDINBURGH

www.luath.co.uk

First Edition 2000

The paper used in this book is acid-free, neutral-sized and recyclable.
It is made from low chlorine pulps produced in a low energy, low
emission manner from renewable forests.

Printed and bound by
Bell & Bain Ltd., Glasgow

Typeset in 10.5 point Sabon by
S. Fairgrieve, Edinburgh, 0131 658 1763

Maps by Jim Lewis

## Dedication

This work is dedicated to the Unknown Soldiers of Cromwell's Republic who fell in the Battle of Tullich near Ballater in 1654, overcoming bands of Royalist bandits under Locheil. When will we see their like again?

# Acknowledgements

I would like to thank Dr Mike Dey of Aberdeen Art Gallery and Museums for his help with the work on the illustrations for this book, twenty of which were originally included in the exhibition we jointly curated at Aberdeen Art Gallery in 1999, 'Scotland's Mountains before the Mountaineers'. His aid in chosing materials from the Gallery's collection was especially appreciated as he was recovering from a serious mountain bike accident at the time. The four further illustrations are taken from my own copy of the first edition of Queen Victoria's *Leaves from the Journal of our Life in the Highlands*. In all quotations from this work, her original (mis)spellings have been retained.

# Contents

# Walks

# A Cautionary Note on the Maps and Walks

THE MAPS INCLUDED IN this book are sketch-maps of the journeys undertaken in the Highlands by Victoria, and are not in any way intended as guides for walkers. Many of the journeys Victoria took are short walks on easy ground, suitable for the average pedestrian – and these are indicated in the text – but others go into wild country where even today roads are bad, weather can be deadly and there are less habitations than there were a century ago.

Any one thinking of undertaking the walks in this book is advised to equip themselves with the relevant Ordnance Survey map (these are indicated in the text), and to be properly shod (Vibram boots) as well as clothed (good waterproofs) and to carry adequate supplies of food, as well as a compass. On her Great Expeditions, Victoria had servants, ponies with hampers and reinforcements posted at stages along the route; you will not have, so be prepared! The estimated times given for the walks cover the range from fit walker to average pedestrian. No responsibility can be accepted for any accident, loss or inconvenience arising.

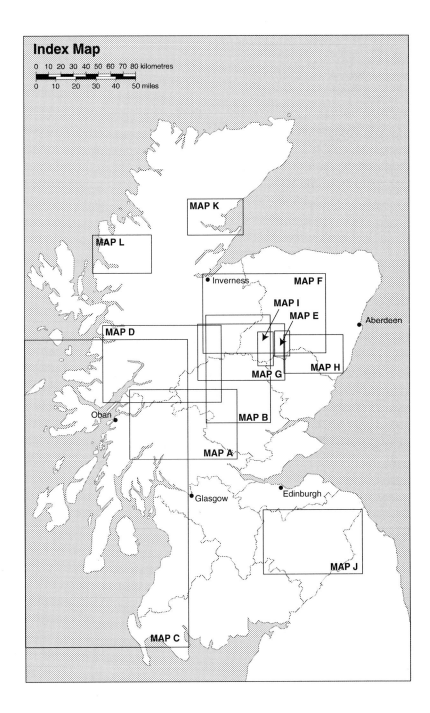

# Index Map

0  10  20  30  40  50  60  70  80 kilometres

0    10    20    30    40    50 miles

MAP K

MAP L

● Inverness

MAP F

MAP I

MAP E

● Aberdeen

MAP D

MAP H

MAP G

MAP B

● Oban

MAP A

● Glasgow

● Edinburgh

MAP J

MAP C

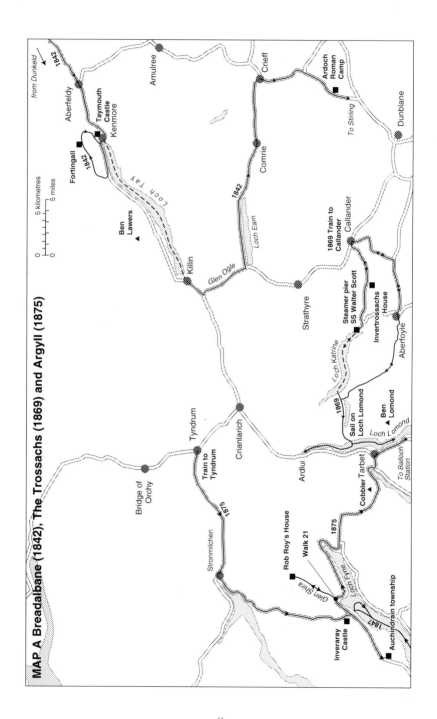

MAP A Breadalbane (1842), The Trossachs (1869) and Argyll (1875)

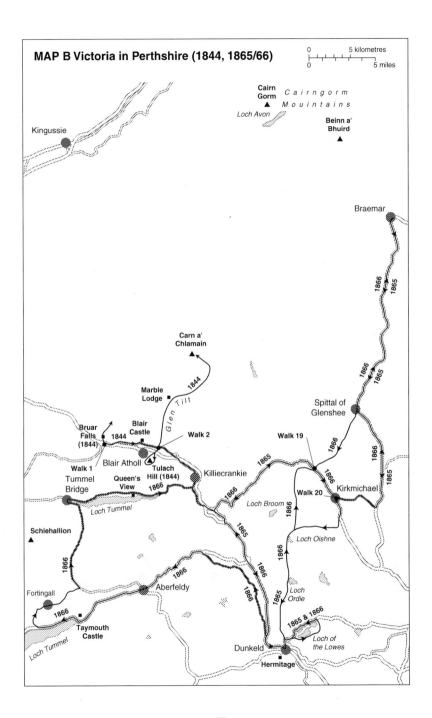

MAP B Victoria in Perthshire (1844, 1865/66)

0    5 kilometres

0    5 miles

Cairn Gorm ▲

*C a i r n g o r m*

*M o u n t a i n s*

*Loch Avon*

Beinn a' Bhuird ▲

Kingussie

Braemar

1866

1865

Carn a' Chlamain ▲

1866

1865

1844

Marble Lodge ■

*G l e n   T i l t*

Spittal of Glenshee

1866

1865

Bruar Falls (1844)

Blair Castle

1844

Walk 2

Walk 19

1866

1866

Walk 1

Blair Atholl

Tulach Hill (1844)

Killiecrankie

1865

Kirkmichael

Tummel Bridge

Queen's View

1866

1866

Walk 20

*Loch Broom*

1866

*Loch Tummel*

1865

Schiehallion ▲

1866

1865

1866

*Loch Oishne*

Aberfeldy

1866

1866

Fortingall

1866

1865

*Loch Ordie*

1866

Taymouth Castle ■

1865 & 1866

*Loch of the Lowes*

*Loch Tummel*

Dunkeld

Hermitage ■

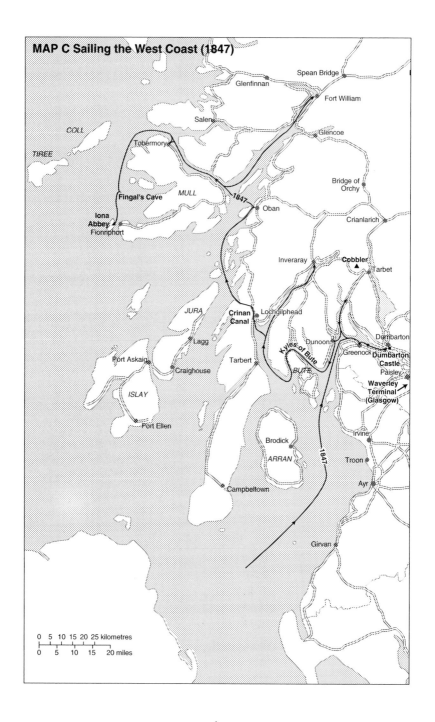

# MAP C Sailing the West Coast (1847)

COLL

TIREE

Glenfinnan

Spean Bridge

Fort William

Salen

Tobermory

Glencoe

**Fingal's Cave**

MULL

Bridge of
Orchy

1847

Oban

**Iona
Abbey**
Fionnphort

Crianlarich

Inveraray

**Cobbler**

Tarbet

JURA

**Crinan
Canal**

Lochgilphead

Lagg

Dunoon

Dumbarton

Port Askaig

Kyles of Bute

Greenock **Dumbarton
Castle**

Craighouse

Tarbert

BUTE

Paisley

**ISLAY**

**Waverley
Terminal
(Glasgow)**

Port Ellen

Irvine

Brodick

1847

Troon

ARRAN

Ayr

Campbeltown

Girvan

0  5  10  15  20  25 kilometres

0    5    10    15    20 miles

# MAP D Lochaber (1847 and 1873)

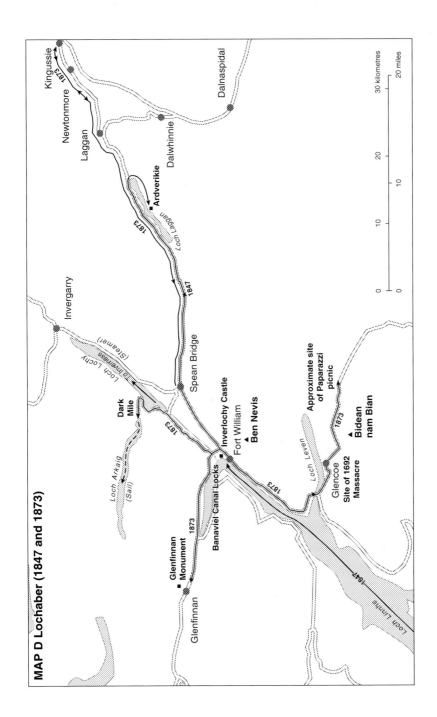

Kingussie
Newtonmore
Laggan
1873
Invergarry
Ardverikie
Dalwhinnie
Dalnaspidal
Loch Laggan
1873
1847
Spean Bridge
Loch Lochy
to Inverness (Steamer)
Dark Mile
Loch Arkaig (Sail)
1873
Glenfinnan Monument
Glenfinnan
1873
Banavie Canal Locks
Inverlochy Castle
Fort William
Ben Nevis
Loch Leven
Glencoe
Site of 1692 Massacre
1873
Approximate site of Paparazzi picnic
Bidean nam Bian
1873
Loch Linnhe
1847

0   10   20   30 kilometres
0   10   20 miles

xv

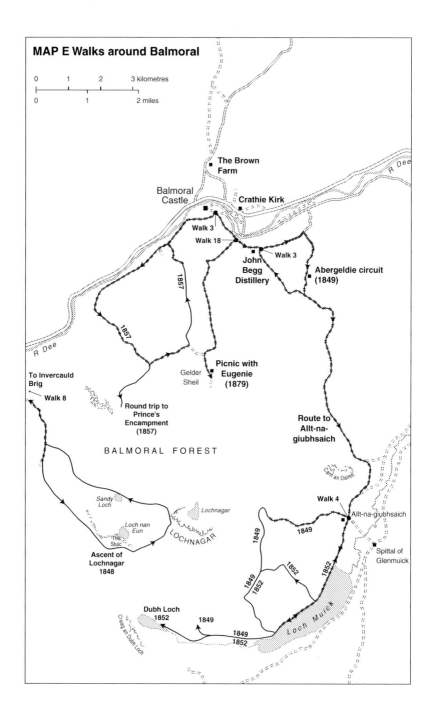

# MAP E Walks around Balmoral

0     1     2     3 kilometres

0          1          2 miles

The Brown Farm

Balmoral Castle

Crathie Kirk

Walk 3

Walk 18

1857

Walk 3

John Begg Distillery

Abergeldie circuit (1849)

R Dee

Picnic with Eugenie (1879)

Gelder Sheil

To Invercauld Brig

Walk 8

Round trip to Prince's Encampment (1857)

Route to Allt-na-giubhsaich

BALMORAL FOREST

Carn an Daimh

Sandy Loch

Lochnagar

Walk 4

Allt-na-giubhsaich

Loch nan Eun

The Stuic

LOCHNAGAR

1849

1849

Ascent of Lochnagar 1848

Spittal of Glenmuick

1849

1852

1852

Dubh Loch 1852

1849

1849

1852

Creag an Dubh Loch

Loch Muick

xvi

# MAP F In and around the Cairngorms

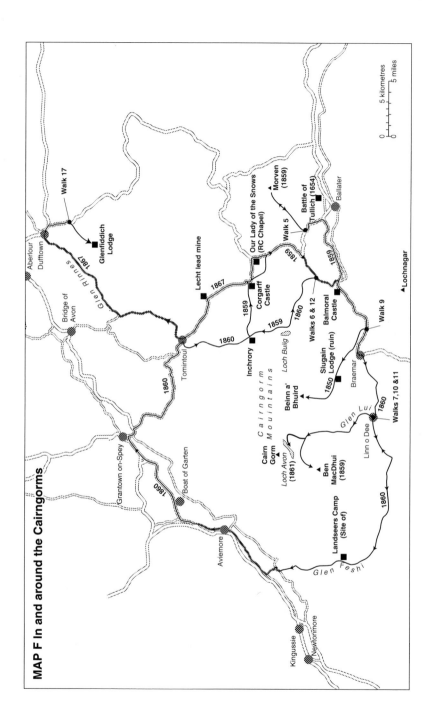

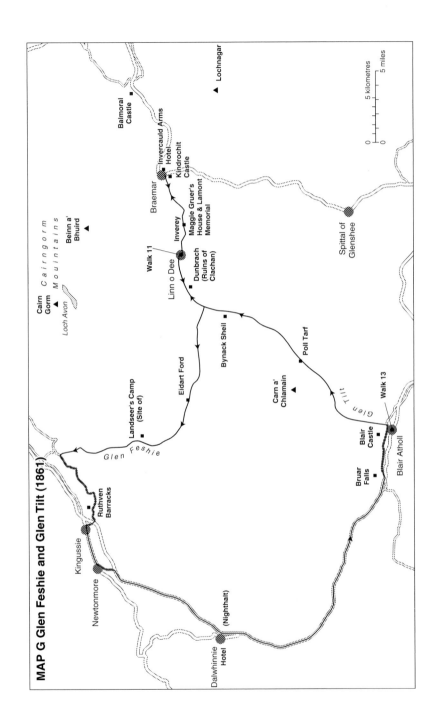

MAP G Glen Feshie and Glen Tilt (1861)

Balmoral Castle

Invercauld Arms Hotel

Kindrochit Castle

Braemar

Maggie Gruer's House & Lamont Memorial

Lochnagar

Inverey

Cairn Gorm

Cairngorm Mountains

Beinn a' Bhuird

Walk 11

Linn o Dee

Loch Avon

Dunbrach (Ruins of Clachan)

Spittal of Glenshee

Bynack Shiel

Landseer's Camp (Site of)

Eidart Ford

Poll Tarf

Carn a' Chlamain

Glen Feshie

Glen Tilt

Walk 13

Blair Castle

Bruar Falls

Blair Atholl

Ruthven Barracks

Kingussie

Newtonmore

(Nighthalt)

Dalwhinnie Hotel

0        5 kilometres
0        5 miles

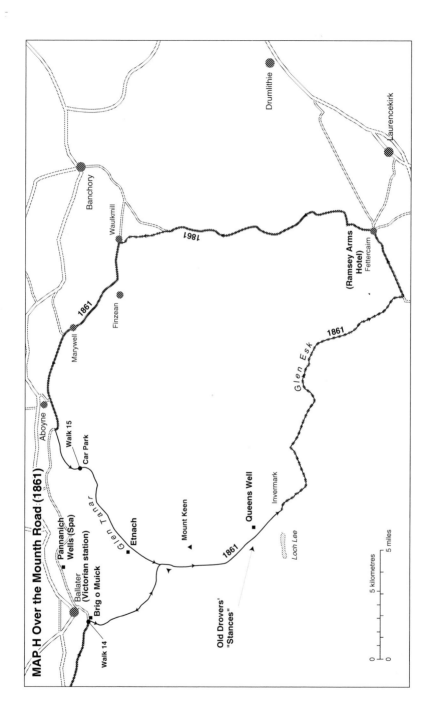

MAP H Over the Mounth Road (1861)

Laurencekirk

Drumlithie

Banchory

Waulkmill

1861

Finzean

Marywell

1861

Aboyne

(Ramsey Arms Hotel)
Fettercairn

Walk 15

Car Park

*Glen Tanar*

*Glen Esk*

1861

Pannanich
Wells (Spa)

Etnach

Mount Keen

Invermark

Queens Well

1861

Loch Lee

Ballater
(Victorian station)

Brig o Muick

Walk 14

Old Drovers'
"Stances"

0        5 kilometres
0                    5 miles

xix

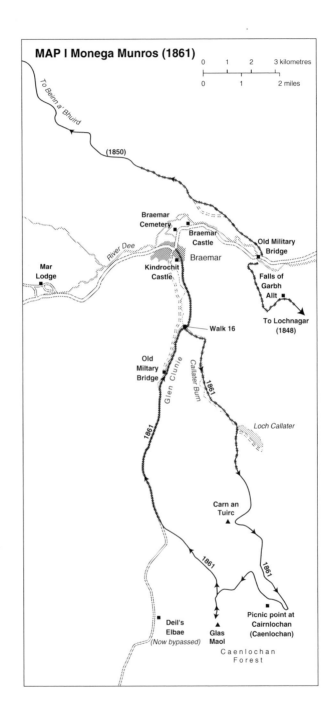

**MAP I Monega Munros (1861)**

0   1   2   3 kilometres

0   1   2 miles

To Beinn a' Bhuird

(1850)

Braemar
Cemetery

Braemar
Castle

Old Military
Bridge

River Dee

Braemar

Mar
Lodge

Kindrochit
Castle

Falls of
Garbh
Allt

Walk 16

To Lochnagar
(1848)

Old
Miltary
Bridge

Glen Clunie

Callater Burn

1861

1861

Loch Callater

1861

Carn an
Tuirc
▲

1861

1861

Picnic point at
Cairnlochan
(Caenlochan)

Deil's
Elbae

Glas
Maol
▲

*(Now bypassed)*

Caenlochan
Forest

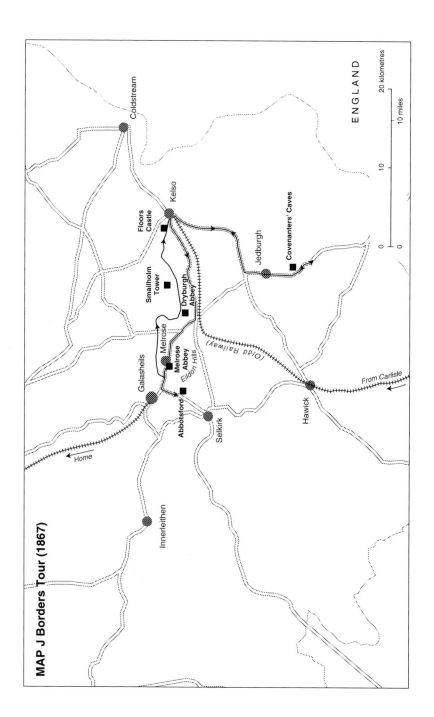

MAP J Borders Tour (1867)

Coldstream

Kelso

Floors Castle

Smailholm Tower

Dryburgh Abbey

Melrose

Melrose Abbey

Eildon Hills

Abbotsford

Galashiels

Selkirk

Innerleithen

Home

(Old Railway)

Hawick

From Carlisle

Jedburgh

Covenanters' Caves

ENGLAND

10 miles

20 kilometres

10

0

0

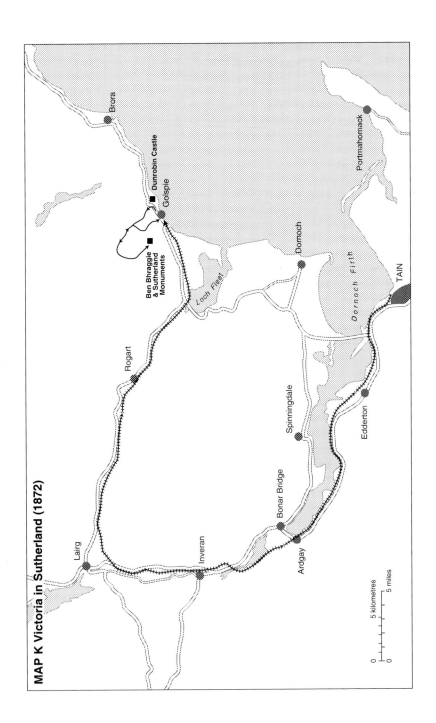

# MAP K Victoria in Sutherland (1872)

Brora

Dunrobin Castle
Golspie

Ben Bhraggie
& Sutherland
Monuments

Portmahomack

Rogart

Dornoch

*Loch Fleet*

*Dornoch Firth*

TAIN

Spinningdale

Edderton

Bonar Bridge

Lairg

Inveran

Ardgay

0    5 kilometres

0    5 miles

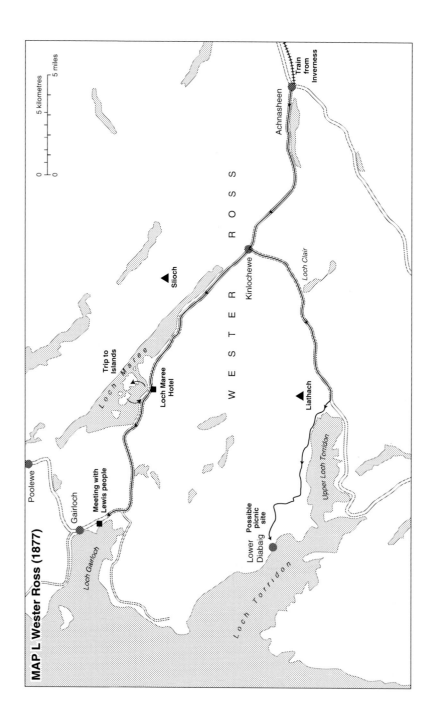

MAP L Wester Ross (1877)

# Bolshevising Balmorality

WHEN GAVIN MacDOUGALL of Luath Press suggested to me that as a mountaineering writer having a lifelong association with the Cairngorms I might like to consider a work on Queen Victoria for inclusion in the Luath *On The Trail of* series, my initial reaction was one of not being amused. How could I, an outdoor author whose writings on the issue of mountains had been described by various critics, depending on their standpoints, as either 'enlivened by' or 'marred by' a Marxist perspective on the issues of land usage, how could I write with any empathy on the peregrinations of Vikki Regina? And yet, I began to think, and yet... possibly the whole issue of Victoria's residence on Deeside, and her tours in the mountains of Scotland, could be explored and exploded from within, in a light, yet serious *Kulturkritik*, in a Bolshevisation of Balmorality. After all, *'It ain't what you do, it's the way that you do it'*. So, facing the prospect of being caught in a crossfire of outraged monarchists and sceptical republicans, I decided to accept the challenge.

The historical reality is, like it or not, that the Cairngorms in general, and Upper Deeside in particular, are associated with, indeed saturated by, the presence of the British monarchy. From the muckle *Schloss* itself at Balmoral to the 'New' Kirk at Crathie, from the cairns and statues which litter the landscape of the royal estate to the ornate 'By Appointment' signs over the butchers', bakers' and candlestick-makers' shops in Ballater and Braemar, one can no more escape the stamp Victoria and her legatees put on the area than one can ignore, for example, the Mormon presence in Utah's mountains. From the historical reality we must start; analyse and criticise it as we may, we do not have the option of 'Not starting from here'. What is on Deeside may be a never-never land, but it is a *real* never-never land!

What it was that possessed the British monarchy to indulge

with such enthusiasm, expense and unself-consciouness in the creation of a neo-feudal fairyland in the mountains, and why this occurred in the epoch it did, rather than at another time, appeared to me be a point worthy of examination. How did this fit in with the self-image of Scotland which was being created in the mid-19th century? Barring the castle-building and Bayreuth fantasies of the mad Ludwig in Bavaria, there is nothing like it, and Balmorality has had a longer and more profound impact than the architectural dreamings of Wagner's patron, now emptied of their Wittelsbach inbabitants. It also occurred to me that there might be parallels with the difficulties of the monarchy in the middle of the last century, and its contemporary dilemmas, which would be worth the making. The soap opera of royal life, which still has chapters staged at Balmoral, did not start with the marital problems of the present heir to the throne, but with the builders of the edifice. Problems with royal sexual scandals, with the paparazzi, and with attempts at positive image-making at a time when the monarchy was under attack, were as much in evidence in Victoria's time as in Lizzie's, as the hugely successful film *Mrs Brown* showed.

Balmoral represented the idealisation of the picturesque and the non-urban in British society. It gave the royal stamp to the feeling, growing with industrialisation, that the real Briton was the thatched cottage country-dweller, or in Victoria's case, castle-dweller, who shunned the ugliness of urban life, and in particular the ugliness and threat of its working class. The most industrialised society in the world wallowed in a sentimentalised, overblown romanticism, of which Victoria's favourite poet, Tennyson, was the supreme example. Another of Vikki's favourite writers was Walter Scott, who is referred to in her *Journals* more than any other author. All the 'feudal rubbish' which the middle classes had been attacking for centuries suddenly became fashionable again, and an idealised version of the organic Middle Ages, with its lines of loyal dependence, came to dominate the culture of Victorian Britain – and other countries, like Germany. Pre-Raphaelite art and music with roots in Catholic medievalism was the intellectual fodder of a middle class which saw the barbarians – in the form of the proletariat – at the gates. Balmorality, with its feudal architecture and feudalised life style, fitted perfectly into all this eclectic obscurantism.

I mentioned Scott. How far was he to blame for all this? Scott had outlined the polarities of Scotland in his novels: the Scotland of the Lowlands – Calvinistic, commercial and scientific, and the Scotland of the Highlands – romantic and Jacobite. Until about 1830 the former image, that of Englightenment Scotland, was the one Scots and foreigners had about the country. Scott presented the polarities, and though his heart was probably in the Highlands, his head was in the Lowlands; it was those who came after who presented his image in such a one-sided manner. A natural selection took place as the century progressed, and the Celtified image, of a Scotland whose true essence lay in the clan system of the Highlands (which had by that time been safely destroyed), took over, drawing inspiration from Scott – and elsewhere. Victoria unambiguously embraced this ideal, her love of the Highlands and its people re-enforcing the Victorian public's wish to see Scotland through Celtified eyes. As she said on one occasion:

'This solitude, the romance and wild loveliness of everything here, the absence of hotels and beggars, the independent simple people, who all speak Gaelic here, all make beloved Scotland the proudest, finest country in the world.'

But this was a Scotland of her imagination – though not solely hers – not the reality of urbanised, industrial Scotland in 1869.

As well as allowing the writer to explore elements of cultural history, I also felt that tracking down Victoria's actual travels (we can hardly call them walks) would allow us to voyage through a physical landscape, not only looking at what she saw and encountered, but also at what she didn't see in the historical and social landscape, and also what she could not see, that is, what was to come afterwards. Even on Upper Deeside, time has not (quite) stood still, and much has happened that readers can ponder on, as they read about the expeditions of the former 'Mother of her People', as the editor of her *Leaves from the Journal of our Life in the Highlands* described her. This editor was the appropriately-named Arthur Helps, Clerk of the Privy Council, who wrote a Preface to the work, obviously with Victoria's approval. The *Leaves*, wrote Helps,

'... illustrate in a striking manner, the Patriarchal feeling (if one may apply such a word as 'patriarchal' to a lady), which is so strong in the present occupant of the Throne.

(No-one) feels more keenly what are the reciprocal duties of masters and servants (or wishes) that there should be no abrupt severance of class from class, but rather a gradual blending together of classes...'

This invention of Victoria as the Mother of the Nation was in part the work of Disraeli, who saw it as a monarchist bulwark against social disorder. And many felt in 1868 that such bulwarks were needed. The Reform Act of 1867 had just been passed, and had been supported by much agitation from the trades unions of skilled workers who largely organised the campaign. The Act had been proceeded by severe rioting in Hyde Park, which caused Karl Marx to exult that 'The English Revolution began yesterday in Hyde Park.' Many on the other side of the fence felt that a 'leap in the dark' with unpredictable consequences had been made. Victoria herself, as we shall see, lived in constant dread of social disorder, and about this time wrote to one of her daughters about the prospect of 'a new French revolution' in Britain. Her *Leaves* were a modest part of the ideological offensive against such a pos-sibility, showing a harmonious world where the social classes could live with 'the reciprocal duties of masters and servants' clearly delineated. My own book is, in turn, a counter-blast to such a perspective.

This work is not a hagiographical exercise in biography of the 'She was a Truly Great Queen' type or one of those genealogically-obsessed works so beloved of the (declining) band of fervent monarchists found on these shores: for those who wish to know everything Victoria wore and ate, and the titles and relations of all the persons who flit across these pages, there are other works to consult. But neither, I hope, is it a hatchet job; despite the misfortune of her birth, Vikki was – put charitably – the best of her bunch, and I'm sure she would have made a half-decent bothy companion, had she had the fortune of another lifetime. What I want to do in the work is to retrace Victoria's main travels, and construct around them an outline of the social and historical landscape of Scotland in the last half of the 19th century. I do not intend to track down every single trip made by the wumman – as John Brown was wont to call Victoria – or every single stone that had the honour to be trodden by the royal foot, but to concentrate on significant journeys. Much of the travelling will be focused on Upper Deeside. These were the most adventurous trips she made, since most of those elsewhere, and after Albert's death, were done by train, or kept to main roads. But those journeys made and described in the second volume of *More Leaves from the Journal of a Life in the Highlands* (1884) will also be considered.

Hopefully the reader will enjoy following in these pages the expeditions of Victoria, and be tempted to undertake at least some of them on the ground – and as much to the point, will ask themselves some of the questions I feel the book poses, such as, is it reasonable that all this beautiful countryside, any more than the wind and rain and rivers and wildlife, can actually belong exclusively to someone, or should its utilisation and care not be the collective responsibility of us all?

*Ian R. Mitchell*
September 2000

P. S. I have adopted a pet-name for Victoria in this work. To any who might object, I say it is between ourselves.

# CHAPTER I

# In search of Brigadoon

IT TOOK VICTORIA A LITTLE while to find her *Brigadoon*, the perfect Scottish place – though some may feel that the land she finally selected, round what the locals would call the *Brigadee* (Bridge of Dee), wakes up rather less frequently than *Brigadoon's* once a century. For if Victoria, Albert, John Brown and the rest of them rose from their long sleep, they would have no difficulty in recognising the country between Braemar and Ballater, so little has it changed. Indeed in some ways the royal presence put the area to sleep socially as well; none of the movements which affected the Highlands from the 1840s onwards had very much impact on Upper Deeside, a point we shall return to when dealing with Victoria's legacy.

Victoria came to the throne of Britain in 1837, at the age of 18, at a time of great social convulsion in the country. On the one hand, the rising middle classes had forced the passage of the Reform Act of 1832, which had begun the erosion of aristocratic power. On the other hand, with the formation of trades unions and the Chartist movement, the working class was beginning to emerge as a social force. In addition, the prestige of the monarchical office, after a succession of degenerates and incompetents as its incumbents, was at a low ebb. Vikki's bum sat uneasily on the throne.

In October 1839, the Prince of Saxe-Coburg, her first cousin, arrived in London. A member of a royal house which ruled a state of 300,000 inhabitants, (a 'Pumpernickel state' as the novelist Thackeray dubbed it), he was hard up and on the look out for a match. 'I beheld Albert, who is beautiful', recorded the Queen in her diary, and she decided to marry him – doing the wooing herself, since it would be unseemly for a Pumpernickel prince to woo the monarch of the most powerful country on earth. Victoria was barely five feet tall and no beauty, but despite this, and the mocking of the cartoonists and the opposition of the Tories, she got her man and married him in 1840. She doted on Albert (although one has to wonder why – she was twice the man he was) and was genuinely hurt at the hostility and disrespect shown him by the press and political establishment. The limits of her power were shown when she wanted him King, and found this was in no way possible.

At first Albert's role was somewhat vague. Melbourne, the Prime Minister, noted that Vikki's man was lazy, something he welcomed since it stopped Albert interfering where not wanted. Initially he did little more than – literally – hold his wife's blotting paper when she signed and wrote letters. But even a cynic like myself has to admit the pair got on well. Victoria wrote of the bliss of the married state, and her bearing nine children possibly indicates that her reputation as sexually restrained was not altogether accurate. The Mother of her People became a firm advocate of chloroform in childbirth – but a fierce opponent of breastfeeding, horrified when one of her daughters adopted the practice.

Albert is usually credited for introducing the Christmas tree to Britain, and little else. However, coming from central Europe, he was much more exposed to the worship of nature and especially mountain scenery than his young bride. German poetry and song of the early 19th century is full of odes about miller-boys wandering in the *Wald*, or in the *Bergen*, and the use of mountains as recreational resources began earlier in central Europe than here. Albert was familiar with German Thuringia and Switzerland as mountain areas, and to the young couple a Mountain Kingdom, away from all the pettiness of London, must have had great appeal – and such they were soon seeking.

Tourism was already a substantial industry in Scotland in the 1840s, and the places of pilgrimage were mainly those made famous by the writings of the Abbotsford Wizard. 'What would this country be without Walter Scott?', asked the German novelist, Fontane, when he visited the country in the 1850s. Like many visitors to Scotland, Victoria's perceptions of the country were formed by literature, and supremely by the works of Scott. She was an avid reader of his poems and novels, and in her *Leaves from the Journal of our Life in the Highlands*, Scott is mentioned more than any other writer – Albert obviously sharing in her passion for his work. By this time Scotland was Scott-land, and the aspects of his works which were image-forming were those dealing with the Celtic, the picturesque, the neo-feudal and the romantic. Victoria was lucky: she was to find what she went looking for, and her writings helped develop and sustain an image of Scotland which was largely unreal, to the extent that when the practical Yank who was looking for a setting for *Brigadoon* came to Scotland a century later, he left disappointed, saying: 'I couldn't find anywhere that looked like Scotland.' Victoria, however, did.

Before settling on Balmoral on Deeside, Victoria made three visits to Scotland in the 1840s. It is interesting to compare her perceptions of the country at that time with the contrasting image of historians – which is not to say that her reality may not be a part of the whole story. The 1840s were the years of the Highland famine, a parallel, though less intense, version of the Irish famine. In central Scotland the decade was marked by the struggles of the Chartist movement, by urban disorders and some very intense strikes in the industrial areas, and by periods of mass unemployment and real hardship. Though Victoria does not concentrate on these aspects of the Scottish scene, some do occasionally intrude at various points in the Monarch's musings.

## *Breadalbane: a Highland Sampler*

A veritable flotilla of ships accompanied Victoria from Woolwich, along the English coast, to unromantic Granton where she first set foot on Scottish soil on 1 September 1842, being met by Sir Robert Peel, the Prime Minister, and the Duke of Buccleuch, with whom she stayed at Dalkeith House. On the 3rd Victoria did the now common tourist circuit of Auld Reekie, driving in a barouche past Arthur's Seat, past Holyrood Palace and up the High Street to the castle, where she viewed the regalia of Scotland. Like many others, she was impressed by the Athens of the North, commenting:

'The impression Edinburgh has made on us is very great; it is quite beautiful, totally unlike anything else I have seen; and what is more, Albert, who has seen so much, says it is unlike anything *he* ever saw.'

Interestingly, the Queen rode, only descending from her carriage at the castle; walkabouts were not the thing in those days, and possibly too, the royal nostrils were being protected from the smells of the tenements and closes on the High Street, which, though picturesque, were at this time among the worst slums in Europe. Victoria observed the poverty of some of the population, noting 'all the children and girls are barefooted', also noting that 'The country and the people have quite a different character from England and the English... Albert says that many of the people look like Germans.' A stand in Bank Street collapsed after they passed, injuring 50 people and killing two: a fitting way for fervent monarchists to go!

After pottering about for a couple of days, she took a steamer at South Queensferry for Fife, giving her thoughts to 'poor Queen Mary' at Loch Leven, before arriving in Perth and passing on to Scone to spend the night with Lord Mansfield. Perth was admired, and 'Albert was charmed, and said it put him in mind of the situation of Basle'. However, next day, en route to Taymouth Castle via Dunkeld and Aberfeldy, the couple saw what they had come for, and the young bride could again, Tammy Wynette style, admire the superior knowledge of her Consort. As they changed horses at *Auchtergaven* (it took *656 horses* to convey the royal entourage to and from Taymouth!), she wrote:

'The Grampians now came distinctly into view; they are indeed a grand range of mountains... Albert said, as we came along between the mountains, that to the right, where they were wooded, it was very like *Thuringen*, and on the left more like Switzerland.'

At Dunkeld there were pipers, and Highlanders with halberds, – as well as sword dancing and luncheon – and when they arrived at Taymouth (which 'lies in a valley surrounded by very high, wooded hills; it is most beautiful'), Lord Breadalbane had prepared a pageant to fit the scenery, with his men drawn up in Campbell tartan, with pipes playing and guns firing. Victoria commented that night as she wrote her diary:

'The firing of the guns, the cheering of the great crowd, the picturesqueness of the dresses, altogether formed one of the finest scenes imaginable. It seemed as if a great chieftain in olden feudal times was receiving his sovereign. It was princely and romantic.'

But it was not 'feudal times', rather industrial Britain in 1842, where the Chartists had just organised the first mass strike in history in pursuit of the vote for working men, a strike accompanied by rioting and several deaths of workmen. O, to be in Taymouth, now the Plug Riots are here!

Ironically enough, the Campbells of Breadalbane, on their 400,000 acres of land, along with the parent branch of their clan in Argyll, had long been 'modernisers', chiefs with strong Lowland connections, and committed to the House of Hanover. On Campbell lands the old clan system was destroyed long before it was in other areas of the Highlands, to be reinvented as pageant in the time of Victoria. History occurring, as Marx said, first as tragedy and then as farce.

If the royal couple's reception at Taymouth was not enough, after dinner there were bonfires on the hills, with a fort in the woods illuminated, and fireworks followed by Highlanders dancing reels to the sound of piping. 'It had a wild and very gay effect,' enthused the Queen, and was a far cry from the life she led in London. She took a sail on another occasion on Loch Tay, mentioning Ben Lawers, which she believed like many then to be 4,000 ft high, and listening to boatmen singing Gaelic songs; again she was reminded of Scott and went on her return to re-read *Lady of the Lake*.

See the proud pipers on the bow
And mark the gaudy streamers flow
...
As, rushing through the lake amain
They plied the ancient Highland strain.

Events like these, repeated when they travelled again in
Scotland, must have been crucial in Victoria and Albert's determining upon the acquisition of a Highland estate. Albert had had
a great time, killing things while 'up to his knees in bogs' as Vikki
put it, adding ever-admiringly that it was 'very hard work on the
moors'. While Albert killed, Vikki went on a wee *Rundfahrt* from
Taymouth to Fortingall and back. At Fortingall she does not seem
to have descended to view either the Roman Camp (now thought
however to be a medieval settlement), or the yew tree in the kirkyard, which was already 1,000 years old when – indeed if – the
Romans arrived.

Victoria's route out of the Highlands took her by Killin and
Glen Ogle, whose scenery especially impressed her 'putting one in
mind of the prints of the Khyber pass'. They came into the
Lowlands at Ardoch, where Albert investigated the astonishing
Roman earthworks – real ones this time. Significantly, Victoria
stayed in the carriage, classical themes interesting her less than
Celtic ones. After visiting Stirling Castle, they left Scotland on 15
September on board the steamship *Trident*. The day before
Victoria had written:

'This is our last day in Scotland; it is really a delightful country,
and I am very sorry to leave it.'

And on ship she added:

'As the fair shores of Scotland receded more and more from
our view we felt quite sad that this pleasant and interesting tour
was over; but we shall never forget it.'

On board the *Trident*, to pass the time Victoria read to Albert
from Walter Scott's poetry. When it had rained at Drummond
Castle she had comforted herself with the Wizard's lays; on Loch

Tay she had been reminded of Scott again; while in Edinburgh a view reminded her of a character in one of the *Waverley* novels. She had come to find Scott-land, and left with her imaginings confirmed.

## An Atholl Browse

Exactly two years later the royal pair set off again from Woolwich, arriving this time in Dundee on 11 September 1844. By the 1840s, Dundee was a textile town with possibly the most savage contrasts of wealth and poverty in Scotland. It was also a centre where Chartism, the movement to gain the vote for working people, was especially radical. But Victoria's interest was not in urban Scotland, and *Juteopolis* is dismissed thus: 'Dundee is a very large place... the situation of the town is very fine, but the town itself is not so.' She obviously didn't like the look of the urban masses either, for she comments that '...as you get more into the Highlands, there are prettier faces'. Ugly, not 'Bonnie', Dundee and Dundonians. The couple quickly headed via Coupar Angus and Dunkeld for Blair Athole (sic) where Lord and Lady Glenlyon awaited them. En route Victoria had tasted Athole brose (a mix of oats, cream and whisky) at a rest stop; she was always willing to try things, and on her earlier visit had pronounced Buccleuch's oatmeal porridge 'very good', and also tried Finnan haddie.

Their reception at Blair Castle was what a royal couple would expect, but not all who came to the area at this time were so fortunate. Lord Glenlyon, later the 6th Duke of Atholl, was turning his estate into deer forest, and was anxious to restrict traditional access. Two locals, one the Episcopalian minister, were walking in Glen Tilt on 19 September and disturbed a hunt organised for Albert. To appease Glenlyon, the minister wrote a grovelling letter of apology. The circuit judge Cockburn recorded in 1846 of Glen Tilt that '...at the lower end of the Glen... he of Atholl has been pleased to set his gates and keepers, and for the same reason that he may get more deer to shoot easily.' This was the beginning of a policy of obstruction continued until very recent times by the Atholl proprietors.

While at Blair Atholl, Victoria and Albert were quite active and engaged in several outings. On the 12th they drove in a pony phaeton up Glen Tilt as far as Marble Lodge, a shooting lodge, marvelling at the scenery and especially *Ben-y-Ghlo* [Beinn a' Ghloe]. Four days later they drove to Bruar, and here the couple were obliged to walk, the path not being suitable for carriages. They walked to the Falls and back, in ecstasies over the mountain scenery whose delight, Albert had obligingly explained to Vikki, 'consisted in its frequent changes'. Victoria shows that she was aware that Burns had preceded her to Bruar and had written a poem asking the then Duke to plant trees, which he subsequently did, but there are few references to Scotland's demotic and republican national bard in her *Journal*.

## WALK 1: BRUAR FALLS (Map B)
### 1 mile, ¼ hour

*Today the walk to the falls and back is a well-laid out, circular trip on good paths. Starting at the House of Bruar, which is an emporium of all things Scottish in tweed and tartan, a signposted path goes to the falls, and can be varied on the return by using a path on the opposite side of the river. (os 43)*

The royal pair were getting bolder, and a couple of days later, in the company of the gillie, Sandy McAra, 'in his Highland dress', they mounted ponies, and then mounted *Tulloch Hill* [Tulach], 'the most delightful, the most romantic ride and walk I ever had'. Though a modest eminence of 1,500ft, south of Blair Atholl, this was Victoria's first mountain and a great experience for her, as she sat admiring the views on all sides. 'I had never been up such a mountain, and then the day was very fine.'

This ascent had obviously fired Victoria to such an extent that a full-scale mountain expedition was planned. In 1844 very few people climbed mountains, apart from locals at their work, or scientists seeking special knowledge; mountain ascents for pure pleasure were very rare, and were to remain so for many years. Once again with Sandy McAra, the party drove up Glen Tilt past Marble Lodge to Clachglas, the house of Peter Fraser, another gillie, on a spectacularly fine day. Here Victoria mounted her pony, and, accompanied by Peter and Sandy amongst others, began ascending by a stalkers' path which she describes as 'very good', to the top of *Ghrianan* hill, wishing she had the artist Landseer with her to depict the scene. The path was in all probability the one up the Allt Craoinidh burn. On Ghrianan Victoria appears to have dismounted and walked to the summit of *Cairn Chlamain* [Carn a' Chlamain]. Here they picnicked and looked over towards the Mar Forest and Deeside, while Albert scurried about in unavailing attempts to kill four footed beasts. The party descended by Sron a' Chro as night was falling, and 'I never saw anything so fine' – recorded the Queen of the sharpening of the hills brought by the fading light.

## WALK 2: CARN A' CHLAMAIN (Map B)
### 16 miles, 6 – 9 hours

*The ascent of Carn a' Chlamain starts just west of the Old Bridge of Tilt, where there is a car park. Taking the good track to Gilbert's Bridge through the wonderful scenery of wood and gorge of the Tilt, you then pass Marble Lodge. Opposite Balaneasie, a good path ascends Sron a' Chro, and height is gained quickly; the ridge along Braigh nan Creagan Breac is followed to the summit. From here the views up the defile of Glen Tilt are magnificent. From the summit, return by the outward journey, or for an organic circuit descend from the summit of Carn a' Chlamain by the splendid stalkers' path, which zig-zags down the mountain-side, reaching the plantation around Forest Lodge; walk back to opposite Balaneasie. (A bike deposited here on the outward journey would be handy.) (os 43)*

Modest as this climb might have been – and though it is difficult to believe than Sandy and the other keepers had not been there already – this ascent by Victoria and party is the first *recorded* ascent of Carn a' Chlamain. (The estate workers certainly knew some of the local peaks: in 1839 a huge bonfire had been lit on the summit of Carn Liath to celebrate Glenlyon's wedding.)

Victoria was now besotted with the Highlands. On 1 October she expressed in her *Journal* her private regret at leaving, a regret she conveyed – with ultimately significant consequences – to Lord Aberdeen on 3 October. She summed up her thoughts.

'There is a great peculiarity about the Highlands and the Highlanders; and they are such a chivalrous, fine, active people. Independently of the beautiful scenery, there was a quiet ... a wildness, a liberty, and a solitude that had such a charm for us.'

Although the only 'Highlanders' they had encountered were lairds and their estate workers, the deferential and hierarchical relations which prevailed on Highland estates appealed to their monarchist sentiments. How this could benefit estate workers willing to observe their deferential and hierarchical roles is shown by the fact that Albert on leaving gave both Fraser and McAra each a gift of £50 for a few days' work – the equivalent of a *year's* wage for a skilled working man at the time.

One relic of this trip was that in 1845 Victoria presented colours to the Atholl Highlanders which gave them the right to bear arms, though rather antiquated ones, and thus become Europe's only private army. The Atholl Highlanders were originally raised as a Volunteer regiment to fight against the American colonists in 1777, but were later disbanded. They were revived as a piece of neo-feudalism by Lord Glenlyon when he went to the medieval games, tournaments and banquetting organised by the Earl of Eglinton in 1839 at Kilwinning, and the Highlanders attended as a private bodyguard for the 'Knight of the Gael' as Glenlyon had dubbed himself. About 150 strong, the Atholl Highlanders' service to Vikki and her romantic notions of monarchy in 1844 resulted in the distinction which they still hold.

# Lochs, Locks and Laggan

Her next expedition, in August 1847, was less energetic than the previous one to Atholl, involving as it did much sightseeing but no ascents and only a few brief outings. The royal fleet sailed to the Scilly Islands, and then past Wales and the Isle of Man into Scottish waters. The couple were in the aptly-named steam yacht, *Victoria and Albert*, which had delayed their initial progress as 'something had gone wrong with the paddle wheel'. (Much of the route of her sail in 1847 can today be re-traced in the paddle-steamer *Waverley*: see Places to Visit.) Victoria was developing a keen eye for mountain beauty, the peaks of Arran including Goatfell being described as 'peculiarly fine from their bold pointed outlines'. After landing at Greenock and visiting Dumbarton to see the castle on the 17th, Vikki and Albert continued their day 'doon the watter' with a sail up Loch Long, where a glimpse of the Cobbler – 'the top of which resembles a man sitting and mending his shoe!' – caused delight, before spending the night at Rothesay. Victoria comments: 'Everywhere the good Highlanders are very enthusiastic.' *Highlanders? Rothesay? Greenock? Dumbarton?* – but I suppose from the deck of a boat any obsequious Scot in a kilt could be construed as a Highlander.

Next day they sailed to Inveraray, where they were met in 'true Highland fashion' by Campbell of Islay and the Celtic Society, with kilts and halberds abounding. Once again her keen eye for mountains had picked out Cruachan, designated 'very fine indeed'. A more realistic aspect of the Highlands in the 1840s was given Victoria the following day, when, after sailing through the Crinan Canal, they passed Coll and Tiree, the latter island belonging to the Campbells. Victoria did not land, but had presumably been informed – as she noted in her *Journal* – that 'The inhabitants of these islands have, unhappily, been terrible sufferers during the last winter from famine.' In 1849, 'in true Highland fashion', the Duke of Argyll shipped 600 people from Tiree to Canada, many of them forcibly evicted, and enduring cholera en route. As was so often the case, the 'loyalty' of the Highlander which Victoria so admired was repaid with a one-way ticket to exile.

Victoria also sailed past the Small Isles, before landing on Staffa and viewing Fingal's cave. She tells us that:

'It was the first time the British standard, with a Queen of Great Britain and her husband and children, had ever entered Fingal's cave...'

They sailed on to Iona where the indefatigable Albert went to see the monastic ruins, and Vikki stayed on board sketching. Stones appeared to leave her cold compared with mountain scenery. From Tobermory they sailed to Fort William, which was the real purpose of their voyage, as they were toying with the prospect of a holiday home in the area. For a couple so young, they were already unduly troubled with aches and pains, and despite the ready availability of opium derivatives at that time, were looking for a place where the climate would be beneficial. Rheumatism as much as Romanticism drove Vikki and Albert to the Highlands.

A century earlier Cluny MacPherson had been one of the most die-hard Jacobites and opponents of the Hanoverian Sucession, living in a cave on Ben Alder as a fugitive after the '45, and entertaining the Chevalier in flight there. A century later, his descendant was entertaining, 'in true Highland fashion', the historical legatee of those who had finally vanquished the Stuarts, in the hope of selling her a chunk of his Highland estate! At this point, the forest of Ardverikie was leased by Cluny to Lord and Lady Abercorn, with whom the royals stayed.

The couple drove in poor weather from Fort William to Laggan where MacPherson and the ubiquitous assemblage of kilted Highlanders awaited, and then went to view Ardverikie, which might, had the weather been better, have been Balmoral. Victoria liked the dramatic scenery round Loch Laggan: 'It is a beautiful lake, ... surrounded by very fine mountains.' The Lodge, with its Landseer drawings, she also liked. (Landseer had often stayed with the Abercorns, but hated the plain whitewashed walls of

Ardverikie which he adorned with the originals of such paintings as 'The Monarch of the Glen' and 'The Challenge'. These were destroyed by fire in 1873.) But she found the place *too* wild. 'There is not a village, house or cottage within four or five miles', she bewailed. But the main negative aspect was the fact that the weather was awful, and she had been informed that on the western coast this was not unusual. She concludes, 'There is little to say of our stay at Ardverikie; the country is very fine, but the weather was most dreadful.' She had stayed the best part of a month before leaving for home on 17 September, having determined against purchase.

On the route south, they passed Campbeltown, which Vikki described as 'a small and not pretty place'. This was a bustling town of distilleries with a shipyard: not her ideal of a Highland town.

**Balmoral**

(from *Leaves from the Journal of Our Life in the Highlands, from 1848 to 1861*, First Edition, 1868)

The rich man at his castle, the poor man at his gate... The contrast between the opulence of the Schloss and the miserable black houses of the peasantry is almost medieval in its stark extreme. But it represents the Brigadoon/Brigadee ideal of a world where masters and servants knew their respective places and duties, a world which Victoria and Albert strove to re-create on Deeside.

**Allt na Guibhsaich, after a sketch by Queen Victoria**

(from *Leaves from the Journal of Our Life in the Highlands, from 1848 to 1861*, First Edition, 1868)

The Queen's 'bothie', with its six en suite apartments, replaced the original sod-roofed house here. After Albert's death, this place became an empty memorial to him, as Victoria moved up loch to the Widow's House at Glassalt Shiel, opened in 1868 – another, even more substantial and comfortable residence to play the bereaved Marie-Antoinette in.

**Fording the Poll Tarf, after a drawing by Carl Haag**

(from *Leaves from the Journal of Our Life in the Highlands, from 1848 to 1861,* First Edition, 1868)

Broon's finest hour as he, given preference over the Chookie Atholl, leads Vikki's pony across the ford. Sandy MacAra is forging ahead at the front with his stick, and Albert is trying to hold his breeks out of the water. The pipers are just managing to keep their drones dry, as the skirl of the pipes accompanies a scene that could be out of the *Morte d'Arthur* or some other medieval romance, as the waters boil, and the mist swirls.

**Luncheon at Cairn Lochan, after a drawing by Carl Haag**

(from *Leaves from the Journal of Our Life in the Highlands, from 1848 to 1861*, First Edition, 1868)

This is actually Caenlochan, and the view is southwards into the Angus glens. What a way to do your mountaineering; ghillies serving wine and food, while you are couched on comfy plaids. Vikki and Albert are on the right, and the latter has his hip flask before him. Victoria said the picnic was at 'a very precipitous place, which made one dread any one's moving back-wards'. Albert missed his chance to give Broon a wee shoudie...

# CHAPTER 2

# 'This Dear Paradise...'

THE SURPRISING THING ABOUT discovering *Brigadoon* at the *Brigadee*, and the leasing of Balmoral, was that after these earlier trips with one eye on the weather and another on the property market, Victoria and Albert decided on Balmoral without ever having visited or seen it! Sir James Clark, the Royal Physician, had originally suggested Scotland as a possible location for a home which would help the couple's health, especially their rheumatism, mentioning Deeside on account of its dry climate. Then Lord Aberdeen, a future Prime Minister, suggested to the Queen that she acquire the lease of Balmoral, which had become vacant on the death of his brother, Robert Gordon. It is not quite true to say that Victoria never saw it before taking the lease. The Aberdeen artist, James Giles (1806-70), travelled to London with his sketches and drawings of the estate and the castle, and these with Aberdeen's recommendation clinched the deal. The estate of over 17,000 acres was eventually bought from the Fife Trustees in 1852 for 30,000 guineas, which allowed work to begin on the new castle. Later, in 1878, Victoria bought Ballochbuie Forest from the Farquharsons, something Albert had failed to achieve – though he had managed to purchase Birkhall and get a long lease of Abergeldie, neighbouring properties. These property deals were helped by the eccentric James Nield leaving the royal couple £250,000 in his will, the most bizarre example of Victorian philanthropy I have come across.

Once the estate was purchased, Albert set about demolishing the old castle and bulding a new one. The old castle wasn't so very old; it had been built by Sir Robert Gordon in the 1830s and his architect was 'Tudor Johnny' Smith, ironically the father of William Smith who was engaged to build Balmoral – though

Albert clearly had a great deal of input into the design of the mongrel cross between a feudal Scottish castle and a German *Schloss*. Although labour disputes occurred amongst the highly skilled and unionised masons on the project, the work went ahead and was completed in 1855. The family entered their new home, and three days later came news that Sebastopol had fallen. Forgetting it was a *French* victory in the Crimean War, this was taken as a providential sign, and was wildly celebrated with whisky, fires and fireworks after the station master at Banchory brought the telegram he had received to Balmoral by horse. The meaningless and merciless waste of life that was the Crimean War was over, though it had cost Lord Aberdeen his career as Prime Minister. Vikki had spent the war in a pitch of patriotic frenzy, punctuated by wishes that she could be Florence Nightingale.

## *Deeside before Balmorality*

Balmoral was not such an off-the-wall choice for a royal residence as might at first appear, for the area had a long direct and indirect association with the Scottish monarchy. Malcolm Canmore, crowned in 1057, can claim to be the first proper king of a united Scotland, and he frequently visited a place called *Doldencha* on Upper Deeside for hunting trips with his English wife, Margaret. Keen on developing the military prowess of the Highlanders, he is supposed to have instituted various exercises and games with prizes for the winners, the forerunner, far distant, of today's Braemar Gathering. The main event was a race up Craig Choinnich (1,764ft) outside Braemar. Robert the Bruce crossed the Mounth to Deeside on his way to Kildrummy Castle on Donside, but it is not possible to ascertain his exact route.

Later documents refer to *Kyndrocht in Marre* where Scottish kings had a castle and hunting seat. Kindrochit Castle stood for many centuries, and today its ruins can be found opposite the car park in Braemar and are worth a visit. On one occasion its inhabitants caught 'plague', and the locals barricaded them in and starved them to a quarantined death – so feudal loyalty was not always evident in the Braes o Mar! Charles II visited Deeside in 1650 during his troubled reign, the last monarch before Victoria to so do. But amidst all this monarchism, there is a consolation for republicans. In 1654 troops of the British Republic ventured out from Aberdeen to deal with bands of royalist counter-revolutionaries on Upper Deeside. At the Pass of Ballater they met, and after a fierce struggle, the Roundheads under Captain Morgan routed 1,500 Highlanders under Lochiel, killing 120 and scattering the rest. This battle was the last time the Highlander is recorded to have used the bow in combat. In my youth I dreamed of leading Red Army detachments against counter-revolutionaries in Upper Deeside... but tales of my actual republican incursions into monarchist territory can wait till later in the book.

Indirect contact with monarchy took place, of course, in 1715 and 1745, when chiefs and clansmen from Upper Deeside attempted to restore the Stuarts to the British throne, though the nearest any Pretender, Young or Old, got to Braemar in either case was Aberdeen. In 1715, the leading advocate of the Jacobite cause was Bobbin Jock, or Erskine, Earl of Mar. Though having huge estates in the Highlands, Mar's was really a powerfully-connected Lowland family suffering pique at their apparent snubbing by the new Hanoverian monarchy which dissmissed Mar from office as Secretary of State for Scotland in 1714. Mar retired to Invercauld, as guest of Farquharson, to plot, and invited several hundred of the disaffected to a large hunting party in the Mar Forest. Over a period of two weeks, lavish feasting and great hunts took place – and much plotting. Finally on 5 September at a place in Glen Quoich known as the Punch Bowl, a huge toast was drunk to the enterprise, and on the next day before a crowd of 2,000, on the site of the present Invercauld Arms, the Stuart standard was raised – only for the knob at the top to fall off which those present saw as a foreboding of disaster. Indeed it was. After much indecision, Mar's forces finally met those of the Government (largely composed of Campbells under Argyll) at Sheriffmuir on 13 November. The battle was indecisive; a later Deeside poet and minister at Crathie Kirk, Murdoch Maclennan, wrote,

> There's some say that we wan
> Some say that they wan
> Some say that nane wan at a man
> But ae thing I'm sure
> That at Sheriffmuir
> A battle there was, that I saw, man.

The battle was followed by repression and transportation of some prisoners to the colonies, but compared with the '45, severity was limited. In 1745 however, there was much less enthusiasm for Jacobitism than in 1715. The two main families on Deeside, the Gordons and the Farquharsons (who had bought Braemar Castle after it was forfeit), declared for Hanover, though some of their smaller cadet branches 'came out' under Farquharson's daughter, nicknamed Colonel Anne. Even then, there was great difficulty in recruiting for the army, and many came only when threatened, like the farmers in Glengairn, who were told that if they failed to appear, a party would be sent 'to burn your Corns and House, and drive away your cattle'. The Deeside recruits fought at Falkirk, Inverurie and Culloden, before being abandoned to their fate by their leader with the words 'Let every man seek his safety in the best way he can.' A month after Culloden the Hanoverian troops swept into Deeside, burning the houses of the gentry who had supported the rising, and carrying out arrests, though most of those condemned for taking part in the rising were subsequently pardoned, or allowed into exile. Troops were stationed at Braemar Castle, leased from Farquharson, and at various outposts where their duties in suppressing Jacobites gradually gave way to hunting down illicit distillers. Braemar and Corgarff Castle on Donside were remodelled – including the building of the star curtain walls – by John Adam, master mason to the Board of Ordnance and elder brother of the famous Robert Adam. The last of the troops left in 1831.

So much for its colourful history; but what was Deeside like when Vikki came to stay? We can get a reasonable snapshot by looking at the New Statistical Account of the 1840s, and the contributions of the two ministers of the Kirk of Scotland based on Upper Deeside. The Rev Archibald Anderson, who contributed the account of *Crathie and Braemar* parish, was a favourite of Victoria, and her local minister till his death in 1866. His text is dated May 1842, and covers one of the largest parishes in Scotland, of almost 200,000 acres. Anderson notes that the population is declining rapidly in the parish: from 2,671 souls in 1751 to 1,712 at the 1841 Census. There is poverty in the parish with about 60 people receiving poor relief distributed from the proceeds of Kirk collections and private donations, amounting to about £90 a year in total, and he admits the real numbers are greater for 'there are still some who feel a great reluctance in making themselves known' for relief. But it is clear that the famine conditions prevailing further west were absent on Deeside. Indeed there was a savings bank in Braemar with a capital of £2,000. Additionally, there was a Friendly Society, dating from 1815, whose 'funds are in a prosperous state'. This supported sick and aged members, widows and orphans with part of its funds, while the residue 'is for the encouragement of the ancient games of the Highlanders', whose annual meeting was held in August. This was the first step towards the Braemar Gathering.

While 'Gaelic is generally spoken throughout the whole parish', Anderson notes that 'very few, if any, of the inhabitants are not well aquainted with the English language'. Actually, Gaelic was replaced by Scots, still very strong on Upper Deeside. Here is a good example of the local dialect: Anderson was a great campaigner against the demon drink, commenting that 'There are three public houses or inns, and their effects on the morals of the people are, in many instances, unfavourable.' One man he frequently chastised for drunkenness was Willie Blair, the fiddler, who often performed at Balmoral as well as more bucolic places. Returning from playing at a dance at a local inn on one occasion,

Willie called at the minister's to pre-empt being summonsed, and spoke as follows: 'I've been ower tae a dance at the Inver, Mr Anderson, and I jist came on my wye haim tha ye micht see me, in case ye sud hear I was waur nor I am.'

Catholicism was on the decline in the parish, partly through missionary activity, and partly through emigration. Most Catholics lived in or around Braemar itself where there was a Catholic church, and they numbered about 400, while there were roughly double that number of Protestant communicants in the parish. The Rev Hugh Burgess, in his account of *Glenmuick, Tullich and Glengairn*, mentioned that there was a Catholic chapel in Glen Gairn and about 360 communicants, while there were almost 2,000 Protestants in the parish. Interestingly, over the previous century the population of the parish had seen no decline, being almost 2,200 in 1841, virtually the figure of 1751. This might indicate that it was more prosperous than its rival riparian parish, although here there were 84 paupers, sharing £60 a year in relief, and a large number of illiterates, 600 in the parish all told, a very high figure. However, as well as a Masonic Friendly Society, a 'circulating library' had been established in Ballater. The town, like Braemar, had a daily post service to Aberdeen, but 'no public coach' as yet.

The industry which was eventually to save Upper Deeside was already apparent lower down the river, as Burgess comments:

'Ballater, though of recent origin, is much frequented in summer by strangers from a distance, on account of the salubrity of the air and the beauty of its scenery' – and of course the parish had the now-famous Pannanich Wells – 'They are all... of a cold temperature, but very agreeable to taste... they are allowed to be beneficial to those affected with gravelly, scorbutic and scrofulous complaints. For the accommodation of the water-drinkers, there are comfortable well-aired lodgings and... a great many people resort to them from different parts of the country.'

Certainly agriculture was not the basis of any real prosperity: of 115,000 acres in the parish, 100,000 are described as 'waste', and Burgess criticises the backward methods of cultivating the rest.

Interestingly, Burgess makes no mention of the use of Gaelic in the parish, which confirms other impressionistic evidence that apart from in the Glengairn pocket (where the inhabitants were Catholic and not his parishioners), the language was all but extinct east of Crathie by the mid century.

This then was the place destined to become 'this dear paradise', and to which Victoria came in 1848. Victoria arrived with Albert at the old Balmoral Castle on the afternoon of 8 September. She found the castle itself 'a pretty little castle in the old Scottish style', and loved the scenery, which in deference to Albert, through whose eyes she strove to see everything, 'reminded us very much of the Thuringerwald' in the Prince's native Germany. She preferred Deeside to the country around Loch Laggan, where she had previously contemplated buying a holiday home, in that it was more prosperous and cultivated. Indeed her delight was so great that she observed: 'All seemed to breathe freedom and peace, and to make one forget the world and its sad turmoils.' This comment is not simply a throw-away one. 1848 was the Year of Revolutions in Europe. The French monarchy had been overthrown, and its king was a refugee in Europe. There were attempts to establish a Republic in Italy, and in Albert's Germany the revolutionary tide appeared to flow unabated. 'How much we talked over those events, day by day and hour by hour' Victoria told one of her daughters after Albert's death. And though obviously concerned with events in Germany, and in Saxe-Coburg in particular, Albert was also worried about the stability of the British political system. 'We have Chartist riots every night', he wrote to a correspondent, and he and Victoria hastily abandoned London for the Isle of Wight in face of expected disturbances during the Chartist demonstration of 10 April 1848. The Chartist leader Ernest Jones wrote to Karl Marx that he had a low opinion of German Princes, due to what he saw as Albert's cowardly behaviour. In addition, Ireland was in open revolt in 1848.

Even at Osborne on the Isle of Wight there were alarms and diversions. Local labourers were called in and armed with pitch-

forks when rumours emerged that a gang of Chartists were march-
ing on Vikki's island home. It turned out they were a merry band
of Oddfellows on a Whitsun outing. Though not in as dramatic a
form as many of the other crowned heads of Europe in 1848,
Victoria was in flight in the Year of Revolutions, and the imagined
patriarchal world of the Scottish Highlands was her refuge.
Victoria had old-fashioned ideas on monarchy and legitimacy,
which must at times have been embarrassing for her ministers to
hear, such as when in 1848 the Prime Minister Lord John Russell,
whose Whigs had initially come to power in the Glorious
Revolution of 1688-89, and who supported German unification
and Italian nationalism, was subjected to:

'I maintain that revolutions are always bad for the country,
and the course of untold misery to the people. Obedience to the
laws and to the Sovereign is obedience to a higher Power, divinely
instituted for the good of the people.'

('Yes, Ma'am' I imagine must have been his weary reply.)

## Short Walks with Albert

At Balmoral over the next thirteen years the pair made many expeditions into the mountains of Deeside. Some of these consisted of
long day trips to climb particular hills, while others were journeys
of two or more days into the wilds. However, Victoria and Albert
also carried out several shorter trips of a less arduous nature, and
many of these are worth describing. A selection follows.

Albert was a peely-wally, 'fushionless craitur', who quickly lost
his good looks, and at forty looked like a man of sixty. He was
frequently ill, or imagined himself so. As well as rheumatism, he suffered from migraine, cramp, insomnia, catarrh and liver problems.
Even the adoring Victoria had to admit that he was a hypochondri-
ac, 'as usual desponding as men really only are when unwell – not
inclined himself ever to admit he is better'. And he was always complaining of the cold – not surprising, since Vikki, subject to hot flush-
es, would generally not allow Albert or any other of the family a fire.

(This may be apocryphal. Such was the Byzantine nature of the royal household that one department cleaned the inside of windows and another the outside. Similarly, responsibility for setting the fire and lighting it was split between functionaries. Inefficiency may have accounted for Balmoral's reputation for coldness as much as Vikki's palpitations.) Albert was constantly complaining of being tired, and it is astonishing that a woman of Victoria's spirit appeared to worship the ground her husband walked on and hung on his every – usually unmomentous – word. Possibly his desire to kill things was Albert's form of compensation. He is always disappearing on walks to hunt some harmless beast, and even on board the royal yacht he bangs away at innocent seabirds. Balmoral was thus heaven to him, giving unlimited scope for his killer instinct in the newly-developing pastime of deer-stalking.

The first stalk, or drive, took place shortly after they arrived at Balmoral for the first time, on 18 September, and was in the Ballochbuie Forest, the party probably going by Connachat Cottage and up the glen between Ripe Hill and Craig Doin (Vikki's *Craig Daign*), whence they scrambled up the hill to 'a little *box*, made of hurdles and interwoven with branches of fir and heather'. While Victoria sketched, Albert manfully waited silently for an opportunity, which soon came, and downed a 'royal' stag to the universal delight of the party.

Another stalk the next year took them to the Abergeldie Forest, to a place called *Geannachoil* by Victoria, but which is Seanchoille (the old wood), or in its corrupted form on the map, The Genechal. Here Albert shot a roe, but the sport was marred by a strange incident, the appearance of an old woman on crutches who 'spoiled the whole thing'. Victoria said she looked like a witch, and the keepers reacted in horror to her arrival, so she possibly had that reputation locally. Victoria's reaction to this incident is interesting: initially annoyed at the woman, then laughing rather uncharitably at the keepers' horror ('very amusing to see'), but mostly showing no curiosity in finding out anything about the woman afterwards.

The Craig Doin area became a favourite beat of Albert's, and this was eventually institutionalised by the creation of a semi-permanent 'encampment' in the area, where the prince would go for several days at a time. On 6 October 1857 Victoria took a trip to see what her man was up to. She rode with (the soon to be famous) John Brown and another gillie over a 'pretty new path' through Corrie Buie, which lies between Ripe Hill and Cnap a' Choire Bhuide, then took the *Feithluie* [Feith an Laoigh], finally climbing 'the very steep ascent' to the encampment, now marked by the Prince's Stone at the *Feithort*.

Victoria was pleased to see that Albert was comfortable: 'The little house, with shelves for keeping a few boxes, (no seat), and a little stove, was not at all uncomfortable' – though even here in the wilds social distinction was maintained – 'There was a second hut for the people.'

They drove through the Ballochbuie and over Craig Doin, Albert once again killing a stag – though his spouse noted, not for the last time, 'Poor Albert was much tired, and had to walk all the time, as he had no pony.'

## WALK 3: ALBERT'S BEATS (Map E)
### 10 miles, 3 – 5 hours and 1½ – 2½ hours

*A pleasant circular walk, which allows these favourite beats of Albert to be seen, could be made, starting from Easter Balmoral, and ascending Glen Gelder, before crossing the Gelder Burn to the south of Ripe Hill. A path branching off left from the land-rover track takes you up the Feith an Laoigh to the Prince's Stone. Back at the land-rover track, another left turn takes you to Connachat, there turning east till the Gelder Burn is crossed again, lower down. Here a right turn will take you back to Easter Balmoral. Another 'beat' walk would start at the Distillery, east of the Crathie car park, and take the road south-east past Buailteach; the first land-rover turning left takes you through a small plantation to the Genechal. Continuing to Balnacroft, a left, west turn brings the walker back to the Distillery. (os 44)*

The area around Loch Muick became a favourite resort of Victoria and Albert, especially after the cottage at Allt na Giubhsaich was fitted out for their comfort. They had visited the place in 1848, and on returning in August 1849, found their little 'bothie' transformed, indeed luxuriously equipped and complete with servants quarters. (Vikki delighted in using Scots dialect words. For example, she always spoke of Crathie *Kirk*, not the horrible anglicised *Church* now common. Her German background probably helped here: German was her first language.) However, accuracy deserted Victoria in using the word bothy for Allt na Guibhsaich. (Like Marie-Antoinette, she was playing with rusticity.) It had been a sod-roofed, one story building, but gentrification had improved it to an establishment of some comfort. The couple had four rooms 'all en suite', forbye one for the maid of honour, and another for her maid. Then, a little apart, there was another house for the other servants, and there was a fair wheen o them!

The duo, with entourage, rode on ponies on a road 'much improved' since the previous visit. Victoria does not say what route they took, but it was probably through Glen Girnock and over the east shoulder of Conachraig. Victoria is sometimes vague with route descriptions, and also found Gaelic difficult, causing further problems, since almost all place names hereabouts were Gaelic. She noted:

'[Albert] took a Gaelic lesson during our ride, asking MacDonald, who speaks it with great purity, many words... but it is a very difficult language, for it is pronounced in a totally different way from that in which it is written.'

From the 'bothie' they walked to Loch Muick, whence they were rowed in a boat to the far end. Vikki was impressed. 'The scenery is beautiful here, so wild and grand, – real severe Highland scenery, with trees in the hollow...' and in the course of the row they caught 70 trout! Seven would be a massive catch nowadays.

The next month, they undertook a more ambitious trip to the head of Glen Muick, and here there are route-finding difficulties which we will try to unravel. This time, we are told, they went via Birkhall, stopping at the Linn of Muick, and arriving at Allt na Guibhsaich after midday. Victoria talks of ascending the hill 'immediately behind the house', and passing over hills 'at a great height', before arriving, via a road that 'got worse and worse', at the *Burn of the Glassalt* [Glas-Allt] They probably therefore ascended the Allt na Guibhsaich burn to the col between Lochnagar and Conachraig, before proceeding along the Monelpie Moss to the Glas-Allt burn. She talks of ascending the Strone hill, which cannot be An t-Sron, but must be one of the projections (*strone* meaning nose) of the White Mounth. They dropped into 'a little hollow immediately above the Dhu Loch' for lunch. This is difficult to identify, but could be that occupied by Loch Buidhe. Here they admired the magnificent Dhu Loch scenery, which contains some of the finest cliffs on the mainland of Scotland. Interestingly, these were already known of, and the Rev Burgess in the previously-cited NSA talks of, 'The stupendous, overhanging cliffs of Craigdhuloch, surpassing in grandeur the celebrated rocks of Lochnagar'. Present-day rock-climbers would agree with the minister, for the Dhu Loch is the scene of some of the hardest summer and winter climbing in Britain. Of the scene Victoria remarks: 'The loch is only a mile in length, and very wild; the hills, which are very rocky and precipitous, rising perpendicularly from it.'

She and Albert then descended to the loch, crossing the Glas-Allt burn with difficulty as there was yet no bridge.

At the loch a boat awaited their return, but on the row back a storm arose, and Vikki became alarmed. So she disembarked and rode along 'a sort of sheep path', which was 'very rough and very narrow' along the lochside to home. One of the gillies, John Gordon, agreed of this road, 'It's something steep, and something rough' – which caused royal amusement. The next year Victoria was to note in her *Journal* that 'A new road has been made, and an excellent one it is, winding along above the lake'. It should be noted that there was a good road on the opposite side of the loch, from the Spittal of Glenmuick over into Glen Clova, the so-called Capel Mounth, a traditional drove road and right of way. At the Spittal there was an inn until about 1850, which succeeded another at Inschnabodart, known curiously as Teetabootie (i.e. 'have a good look around') in Scots. Upper Glen Muick was not altogether an unused wilderness pre Balmorality, and the Capel Mounth was crossed by Jacobite forces going to Killiekrankie and retreating from Culloden. Latterly the Spittal was a sheep farm, as I remember it in the 1960s.

In September 1852 the duo were off to the Dhu Loch again, despite news having come that morning that the Duke of Wellington had died – Vikki expressed some pious sentiments, and then went out for a ride. They went along the loch until they came to the Allt Dearg burn, 'up this a winding path has been made', and they took it to the *Moss of Mon Elpie* [Monelpie Moss], and continued along a path where 'the walking is excellent, so hard and dry', to a point where they began to descend to the *Glassalt*, 'along another path which has been admirably made', and descended to the *Shiel of the Glassalt*, 'lately built', for luncheon. Of this part she notes: 'From here it is quite beautiful, so wild and grand. The falls are equal to those of the Bruar at Blair, and are 150 feet in height...' Afterwards they proceeded to the Dhu Loch by the Stullan Burn 'along a beautiful path', but news came confirming Wellington was dead. Vikki mourned, the heavens dutifully opened and 'Our whole enjoyment was spoilt; a gloom overhung all of us.' She predicted there would not be a dry eye 'in the whole country' at the news – not so, if the man who had written the following lines about 1820 was still alive.

The Levellution has begun
I'll go home and get my gun
And shoot the Duke of Wellington.

The next month Vikki had recovered enough from her sorrow at the Duke's passing to write, 'Every year my heart becomes more fixed in this dear Paradise, and so much more so now that all has become my dear Albert's creation.'

## WALK 4: AROUND LOCH MUICK (Map E)
### 8 – 12 miles, 3 – 6 hours (acc. to route chosen)

*A walk can be made in the form of a Rundfahrt, which covers most of this territory around Loch Muick. Take the well worn path to Lochnagar westwards through the woods from Allt na Guibhsaich, until you are below Conachraig, then follow the track southwards over Monelpie Moss, which can be very wet. Crossing the Glas-Allt high up, descend the path past the splendid waterfall to the Glas-Allt Shiel. You can head back to Allt na Guibhsaich from there, but adding adventure to your day, it is worthwhile to take the reasonable path to the foot of the Dhubh Loch, and admire what must be one of the most spectacular pieces of rock architecture in Britain. It is possible to vary the return from Glas-Allt Shiel, by taking the path round Loch Muick to its south side, and coming back to the Spittal, where you have probably left your car anyway. There is a proposal to close this car park, and replace it by a regular shuttle bus service from Ballater. Allt na Guibhsaich and the Glas-Allt Shiel are still royal residences; the Spittal is a Mountain Rescue Post and Nature Reserve headquarters. There is also a toilet (which is ridiculous – walkers should be encouraged to disperse their waste beneficially, rather than concentrating it in damaging locations). (OS 44)*

Albert had to find something to do, to justify his existence and that of his brood to the general public, and patronising the advance of industry and science was seen fitting. His role in the Great Exhibition of 1851 is so well known as to be not necessary to recount here; and this was a role he continued to pursue. On 14 September 1859, Victoria was 'very low spirited at my dearest Albert' having to go off and attend the British Association for the Advancement of Science meeting, held that year in Aberdeen.

What's a girl to do when her man is away? Never one to hang about, Vikki decided to get in tow with her devoted Brown and bag a Corbett, in this case Morven. The party went by the Gairn and 'along a good new road' to Morven Lodge. Here the local keeper joined them and guided the party, and there was the usual picnic, sketching and walkabout half-way, after which ponies were resumed to the summit. Morven is a fine, isolated viewpoint, and Victoria could discern many of the mountains she had ascended. The day was fine, and 'the view from [the summit] is more magnificent than can be described' – as well as Mount Keen and Lochnagar, ships on the sea by Aberdeen could be seen. Surprisingly, Vikki doesn't mention that 'dear Albert' was in that place, possibly since she was enjoying her chat with Brown so much.

One thing Broon probably did not tell her, since he doesn't seem to have had that kind of knowledge, was that the eastern slopes of Morven, near the Burn o Vat, had been the haunt of a notorious outlaw with a MacGregor connection. In the early 17th century, the Marquis of Huntly was troubled by marauders and bandits in this area, so he unwisely invited Patrick Gilroy MacGregor, known as Gilderoy, to police the area for him. This he did well, stamping out all local bandits, but assuming their lawless role himself. During a wedding in the area, he and his men plundered and burnt every defenceless farm, all the occupants being at the celebrations. As the couplet has it,

Culblean was brunt and Cromar herriet
An dowie's the day John Tam was merriet

Eventually captured by Forbes of Craigievar, Gilderoy was hanged in 1658.

On descent from Morven there was tea and cakes at the lodge, and a fire, before the drive home, when Victoria again bemoans the absence of 'my darling Husband'. That evening she was reassured when she received a telegram saying Albert was fine, and while waiting the next day for him, ascended Lochnagar again. She doubtless believed, as would Albert himself, his report that all the savants were 'delighted' with his speech; 'the reception was most gratifying'. Indeed, they wished for more, and on the 22nd a party of the scientists came out to Balmoral, for a fête. They watched a series of Highland games, Highland dancing, and bagpipe playing, all performed by 'the Highlanders in their brilliant and picturesque dresses'. Again Victoria was delighted to hear praise of her 'beloved Albert's admirable speech, [and] the good it had done...'. One wonders what good that could have been?

Science and Balmorality are here seen combining to legitimise the social order.

## WALK 5: MORVEN (Map F)
### 9 miles, 3½ – 5 hours

*Morven can be climbed in a not too strenuous day, by following the route taken by Vikki from the road end at Lary farm; but don't expect tea and cakes at the lodge. (OS 37)*

Given her sex, her epoch and her social status, no-one can accuse Vikki of lacking an adventurous spirit and willingness to thole some discomfort in pursuit of her ecstasies at the mountain scenery. However, it would seem that the short walks and mountain day trips, while enjoyable, lacked a certain spirit of adventure, and the day expedition to Inchrory on 30 September 1859 points forward to her later Great Expeditions furth of Balmoral.

They drove up Glen Gairn, 'passing the farms of Blairglass and Dall Dounie'. This trip was quite an adventure, since once they had passed Corndavon Lodge and arrived at *Loch Bulig* [Builg], and transferred to ponies, they were heading into the unknown. They rode along a burn 'of which no one knew the name; none of our party ever having been there before.' (It was the Builg Burn.) This shows that even people like Brown had a fairly localised topographical knowledge – and OS maps were still quite a way away. They descended to Lord Bentinck's shooting lodge at Inchrory, which had been a military outpost against Jacobites and smugglers after the '45. 'It was the most dismal country I ever saw', wrote Captain Edhouse then, 'full of bogges', and they caught few malefactors, as ' the Inhabitants were up in their sheilings, five or six miles up in the hills'. Here the scenery to Victoria was, by contrast, 'most beautiful' – but they were at a loss as to their directions. Vikki was unperturbed, but in her own words 'delighted to go on *à l'improviste...*'.

At Inchrory they asked directions, and were told that a road went back to the Gairn by Cock Bridge ('a small, straggling, *toun...*'), and after lunching, they headed off in that direction. Along the Don and in the shadow of Brown Cow Hill they passed, and soon were climbing the old military road built in the 1750s 'over some poor and tottering bridges', arriving back at Gairn Shiel in Glen Gairn in the dark. During the journey Victoria admired Brown's 'vigorous, light, elastic, tread which is quite astonishing' and enabled him to move at five miles an hour. Later she said Brown led her pony 'at an amazing pace' up Glaschoil Hill – she admired rugged manliness, did Vikki. Thoroughly enjoying her trip, she commented in her *Journal* 'How I wish we could travel

## WALK 6: TO LOCH BUILG AND BEYOND (Map F)
### 24 miles, 8 – 12 hours

*This is a fine walk, steeped in history. Start and finish at the military bridge over the Gairn, built by Caulfield about 1750, and be prepared for a long, hard day. The bridge still carries traffic after 250 years – that is value for money! Take the path to Tullochmacarrick, and then cross to the south side of the river, following the good path to the ruins of Daldownie (Dall Dounie), and then crossing another bridge to reach Corndavon Lodge, now in ruins. At Loch Builg don't look for the boathouse still marked on the OS It is gone. (I slept in it in the 60s, and have at home a forlorn slate I found at the site.) Descend the Builg Burn by a good stalkers' path, past lovely wee waterfalls and wooded glades, to Inchrory, a palace of a shooting lodge, once owned by the Wills tobacco family, and now ostentatiously protected by a massive deer fence. Turn east to Lagganauld, where Vikki had her picnic; it is a lovely spot, and would suit your own – you will probably need it by now. Passing east below the Broon Coo Hill, you might see the Broon Coo's Fite Caffie, a semi-permanent patch of late snow on its northern slopes. At Delnadamph don't look for the Lodge, for it has been demolished, and used to fill in the lochan also marked on the map. Back at Corgarff is the wonderful castle, whose curtain wall was added when it became a military garrison. It is open. Go and see it. Passing further along the road for half a mile, you come to the old military road, which crosses the tottering bridges mentioned by Vikki. When I was there in 1998 they were being repaired, but what was left of the military road was being destroyed by the repair works! You reach the A939 with another three or four miles to go to get back to your car, and will doubtless look pathetic and hope for a lift. (OS 36 and 37)* about in this way, and see *all* the wild spots in the *Highlands*.' The seeds of her subsequent longer expeditions were sown.

A fine walk this, but a sad one. Along much of the route are ruins of former habitations, especially in Glen Gairn and the Corgarff area, both of which have suffered massive, and continuing, depopulation. A brief influx of population was caused when a silver mine was opened on the Craig of Proney, and Cornish miners were brought in to work it; it closed in 1874.

The last long day expedition Victoria and Albert engaged upon was on 28 September 1861, to Loch Avon. Small beer, for by this time they had begun their proper Great Expeditions. They drove to Castleton (Braemar), 'Grant and Brown on the box, as usual', and to the Derry, remarking that 'the road up Glen Luie very bad indeed', and transferred to ponies as far as where the Etchachan path branches off. But instead of turning, they continued northwards on the Lairig an Laoigh path, which she describes as 'a dreadfully rough, stony road, though not steep, but rougher than anything we ever rode on before, and terrible for the poor horses' feet'. She passed the *Dhoolochans* [Dubh Lochan], and thereafter a little confusion reigns as to the route.

Victoria says they dismounted and went on rough ground for two miles, to where 'We saw the spot at the foot of *Loch Etchan* [Etchachan] to which we scrambled last year, and looked down upon Loch Avon' – which enraptured her – 'nothing could be grander and wilder – the rocks are so grand and precipitous, and the snow on *Ben Muich Dhui* had such a fine effect.'

At length they lunched 'behind a large stone a little above the loch', before returning homewards via Mar Lodge. They would appear to have crossed the shoulder of Creag Dhu and contoured to the vicinity of Etchachan, then descended, possibly to the Shelter Stone itself for lunch, later returning higher up, although still below the summit of Beinn Mheadhoin.

The Shelter Stone and Loch Avon was a common pilgrimage spot for artists, seeking its natural beauty. Fennel Robson, and later Landseer, visited the place, as did plain tourists and such as Gladstone during his stay at Balmoral. But the area had been long known to local people, if only as a place to avoid, since a gang of robbers had traditionally used the Shelter Stone as a base from which to prey on passers-by, such as drovers using the Lairig an Laoigh. Pacification had made such *caterans* a thing of the past, though the hills still provided sanctuary in Victoria's time for a slowly diminishing breed of poachers and illicit distillers. Poaching was actively pursued on Deeside till late into the 19th century, and exchanges of fire could take place; a poacher killed a policeman pursuing him on the Speyside part of these mountains towards the very end of Victoria's reign.

On Deeside, there had been a still of long standing at Balmoral, run by 'Strowan' Robertson the miller as a profitable side-line, and apparently the Redcoats at Braemar were among his customers. Later, the illicit still of John Begg at Richarkarie provided the contraband, but eventually John 'went legal' after the Act of 1821, and in 1845 founded the Lochnagar Distillery. Three years later Victoria visited the place and gave her approval to its works, hence the appellation of Royal Lochnagar to what is a fine malt. However, distilling still went on outwith the law in Victoria's time; indeed the 'vrichts and measons' working on the building of Balmoral Castle were good customers for the illicit trade, maybe helping explain why they threatened strike action during the construction.

## WALK 7: LOCH AVON (Map F)
### 22 miles, 8 – 12 hours

*I would suggest a little variation in this walk, to make it more organic and satisfying, though devoted monarchists can follow in Vikki's precise footsteps. Follow the Lairig an Laoigh as far as the Dubh Lochans, and descend to the Fords of Avon; but do not cross, especially when the water is high. There is no need to anyway, for taking the rough ground on the south of the river and of Loch of Avon, you will arrive at the Shelter Stone, unmistakable in its magnificence. Lunch and read the Visitors' Book. Ascend the burn behind the Stone, heading southwards to Loch Etchachan, and then descend on the good, if eroded, path past the Memorial Hut (an open shelter) and back to Glen Derry. Between the Fords of Avon and Loch Etchachan this is a pretty rough walk, which is why I suppose the royal ponies were not taken that way. For once, relying on Shanks's Pony is an advantage. This walk starts and ends at the Linn o Dee car park. (OS 36 and 43)*

CHAPTER 3

# The Monarch's Munros

SANDWICHED IN SCALE BETWEEN her short walks with Prince Albert and her larger scale Expeditions were Victoria's days out on the mountains. In the course of these she climbed the three most notable summits on Upper Deeside: Lochnagar, Beinn a' Bhuird and Ben MacDhui. Even without the comfort of Vikki's sociable, (an open four-seat carriage, with seats facing, and a coachman's box), her retinues of strategically placed servants, and her ponies laden with picnic hampers, these are walks that are quite feasible in a day for reasonably fit walkers, whose enjoyment will be enlivened by a knowledge of her own experiences and of the historical landscapes of these trips.

## *Dark Lochnagar*

This mountain, which lies on the Balmoral estate itself, was known earlier as Ben Chichues, Hill of the Breasts, because of its shape, and a variant of this, Benchinnans, was still used in some sources into the 19th century. However, the re-naming of the mountain as Lochnagar owes nothing to Victorian (or to Victoria's) alleged prudery, as the current, alternative name to the mammary variant was used from the middle of the 18th century, and is the one found in Byron's poem on Dark Lochnagar. The Scottified name, Meikle Pap, subsequently became applied to one of the peaks of the massif, so no prudery there either. The mountain is a well-loved one in the North-East, as the following rhyme indicates.

> Fecht for Britain? Hoot awa!
> For Bonnie Scotland? Imph, man na!
> For Lochnagar? Wi crook and claw!

After the Jacobite Rebellion the government investigated the mineral and vegetable potential of the Highlands, and one James Robertson climbed the mountain he called *Lochnagan* in 1771, noting that 'a variety of crystal' was found on it; he also noted the 'rocks formed into inaccessible pinnacles'. It was climbed again by the Rev George Skene Keith in 1810 on behalf of the Board of Agriculture; he measured its height barometrically at 3,800ft, a pretty close verdict, but was dismissive of its agricultural potential. Later William MacGillivray, umquhile Professor at Aberdeen University, scoured its slopes for information on flora and fauna; a drenching and exposure on the mountain helped hasten his early death in 1852. MacGillivray made the first descent of the unmistakeable feature now called the Black Spout, today a common and spectacular means of ascent, though not difficult except under snow.

The ground between Balmoral and Lochnagar was once dotted with several settlements, cleared in the 1830s to make way for a deer forest by Sir Robert Gordon, brother of Lord Aberdeen, later one of Victoria's Prime Ministers. *Ruighacail, Rachaish, Buailtaich*. Their remains can still be discerned as grass-grown piles of stone. One of the departing cottars threw a curse at the laird, swearing he would never prosper and have poor luck shooting. The latter indeed proved true, for he was famed for his poor shooting, and Sir Robert later died when a fishbone stuck in his throat. In Deeside, as elsewhere, resistance to eviction was muted, though those remaining often took out their frustrations in another way: poaching. One of the better known poachers' ballads, 'The Braemar Poacher', composed a little before Victoria's arrival on Deeside, mentions Lochnagar as poaching terrain, where the poacher, Grewar (or Gruer), had often had luck, taking game and eluding the keepers:

I am a roving Highlander, a native of Braemar
I've often climbed the mountains, surrounding Lochnagar
I've often roamed the valleys in spite of all command...

What happened to Grewar when, like Victoria, he moved his attentions across the valley to Beinn a' Bhuird, we will discover later.

Victoria arrived with Albert at the old Balmoral Castle on the afternoon of 8 September 1848, and even on her first day she mentions 'the beautiful hills surrounding *Loch-na-Gar...*' and this initial impression remained with her; she later described the peak as 'still the jewel of all the mountains here'. And after just over a week's residence, she decided to climb it, an experience she was to repeat more than once. She did not on this first occasion ascend the mountain by any of the favoured routes used today, and her description lacks exactness – as she said elsewhere 'my head is so very ungeographical' – but it is possible to outline, more or less, her ascent and descent.

Victoria and Albert drove five miles in a post-chaise to a bridge in the Ballochbuie woods; this was almost certainly the old military bridge of Invercauld, where they were met by MacDonald, 'a keeper of Mr Farquharson's as a guide', and others of 'our faithful Highlanders', with ponies and 'our luncheon in two baskets'. These others included Grant, then head-keeper on the Balmoral estate, soon to be a semi-permanent fixture on hill trips and described as 'most devotedly attached to the Prince and myself'. They went through 'the beautiful wood' for about a mile, and then crossed 'a stony little burn', probably that of Glenbeg. While Victoria rode and 'walked a bit', Albert rushed off to shoot at some deer, which he missed, and then at some ptarmigan, bagging a brace. Like many then and since, Albert equated a love of nature with killing it. Victoria says there was 'no road', but the ground was 'not bad' on this part of the ascent.

From here on the route given by Victoria is a little vague, possibly due to the mist descending, but it was clear enough at one point for the party to look down 'on two small lochs called *Na Nian*, which were very striking, being so high up in the hills'. These are Lochan nan Eun (Loch of the Birds) and its neighbour, Sandy Loch, which means that Victoria almost certainly crossed the Stuic peak on her way to Lochnagar's summit, whence one does indeed look down on the lochs. This makes her most likely route of ascent up the Allt a' Choire Dhuibh once she left the Ballochbuie woods, which would take her up the Stuic shoulder. In thickening mist they dismounted, and crossed the plateau to the summit where they had some luncheon. They had taken four hours on the ascent, and Victoria remarks that for the summit push 'Albert was tired, and remounted his pony' – an observation she made frequently about her beloved.

After twenty minutes shivering in the cold and damp, they began to descend, with the weather worsening, 'the wind blowing like a hurricane, and the mist being like rain...'. Albert had come up to the plateau 'by a shorter way' according to Victoria, and that route they took on the descent. This was steeper, and the party 'walked some way till I was quite breathless'. I would think that this indicates a descent from the summit towards the Sandy Loch, as Albert's steeper and more direct route. On descent, the weather cleared and they descended to Ballochbuie in the sunshine, which allowed Victoria a view and Albert another opportunity to blast away. A little sylvan interlude was provided by a walk through the woods from the path to the Falls of Garbh Allt (the Rough Burn), where 'The rocks are very grand, and the view from the little bridge, and also from a little seat lower down, is extremely pretty.' The Ballochbuie forest, known as 'the bonniest plaid in Scotland', and one of the largest remnants of Scots pine forest, was bought by Victoria from the Farquharsons in 1878. Thence they went back to Invercauld. From the bridge, they drove back to Balmoral, where her physician and Lord John Russell were anxiously waiting for them. Thus, with Lochnagar, Victoria had bagged her second Munro, following Carn a' Chlamain in 1844.

Once the royal pair had purchased the Balmoral estate outright, strict rules were enforced to protect their privacy. All tenants were forbidden to let their homes or take in lodgers, though this restriction was common on Deeside estates at this time. Using an Act of Parliament of 1835, the Right of Way which went through the grounds of the estate was re-routed in 1857. The *glasnost* which the monarchy has attempted to introduce in recent years, as a consequence of its troubles, has led to the *Schloss* being open to the public – at a price. But the Royals are no longer above criticism, and there have been accusations that the conservation record of the estate is one of the least satisfactory in the area, and anger has been expressed at its management's application for forestry grants from the public purse.

Doubtless the reader will ponder this and other issues, if he or she decides to climb Lochnagar from the old Invercauld Bridge, thus avoiding the legions of walkers who ascend the mountain by its normal route from the Spittal of Glenmuick. Also worth pondering is that fact that the beautiful bridge, built in 1752 and attributed to Caulfeild, was constructed by Victoria's predecessors in order to help suppress a region notoriously Jacobite in its sympathies. When Victoria came to Balmoral, the monarchy was still unloved, and the Hanoverians still sat a little uneasily on the throne.

Visitors to Balmoral often ascended Lochnagar, though the purported ascent by the Conservative Prime Minister Disraeli in the company of John Brown, depicted in the film *Mrs Brown*, is apocryphal. Dizzy hated Balmoral, which he described as being 600 miles from civilisation, and spent many of his trips there ill. On one occasion he wrote 'I have not been well here... All is ascribed to my posting in an open carriage from Dunkeld to Balmoral'. Vikki eventually excused him attendance. Dizzy's great rival, the Liberal Prime Minister Gladstone, fared much better. A prodigious walker, he was often late in attendance on the Queen due to his tramps – a fact which annoyed her. He did a 19-mile walk up and down Lochnagar, though without reaching the summit, giving as the reason, 'Mist there was and rain to boot. I find the resemblance to Snowdon rather striking. It is 3,800ft; we went up 3,300ft.'

Taking Victoria's route will probably have the advantage of giving you the mountain to yourself, as the Glen Muick routes of ascent are those overwhelmingly used on a mountain which quickly became the most visited on Deeside. Its accessibility to pedestrians, however, was only slowly matched by its attraction for rock

### WALK 8: LOCHNAGAR (Map E)
### 12 miles, 5 – 7 hours

*The bridge at Invercauld (Historic Scotland) is closed to traffic but open to pedestrians, so cross it and take the path through Ballochbuie to the Falls of Garbh Allt, viewing them either on the way out or back. A path continues southwards through the wood onto the open moor; when it ends the going is, as Vikki noticed, not hard up the shoulder of the Stuic. (Thence you will probably want to take a short diversion south to the Munro of the White Mounth.) A good path leads eastwards to the twin summits of Lochnagar, the highest one being the little one (beag), not the big one (mor). Descending to the Sandy Loch requires only a little care, and thence the burn issuing from it can be followed back to Ballochbuie. Or you can simply retrace your outward steps. (OS 44 and a tiny bit of 43)*

climbers; apart from odd routes like Eagle's Ridge, it was only really after 1945 that Aberdonian climbers like Patey and Brooker developed the fabulous cliffs of Lochnagar.

## The Table Mountain: Beinn a' Bhuird

Unlike Lochnagar, the Mountain of the Tables is not readily visible from the Deeside road. It lay in Victoria's day on the march between the estates of the Duke of Fife and Farquharson of Invercauld, though its fine corries were in the latter's lands. The Farquharsons, like many Deeside lairds, had been Jacobites and thrown their weight (albeit reluctantly) behind the Earl of Mar in 1715. The famous hunting party which culminated in the treasonable drinking of punch at the Quoich possibly took place on Beinn a' Bhuird itself.

Noted as *Bini-Bourd* on Robert Gordon's map of 1654, Beinn a' Bhuird, Scotland's Table Mountain, had its first recorded ascent at the hands, or feet, of Rev Dr George Skene Keith in 1810, working for the Board of Agriculture. Keith barometrically ascertained its elevation at 3,940ft, an over-estimation of only 16 feet. Unimpressed, he described the mountain as 'an immense mass, without beauty or fertility'. Shortly afterwards, the mountain was visited by Grewar, the subject of the ballad 'The Braemar Poacher'. He had a less successful day on the hill.

> One day I went tae Ben a Bourd, my gun intae my hand
> Soon there follaed aifter me six keepers in a band
> They swore they would lay hands on me, but I seen let them know
> I was the roving Highlander, would prove their overthrow.

Grewar was taken, despite his bravado, and sentenced to exile in Van Diemen's land, though this was later commuted to imprisonment in Scotland. MacGillivray, the naturalist also climbed the mountain in 1819, and, unlike Keith, was impressed, saying of the summit panorama: 'The scene presented here I considered... the most noble without exception which I had ever seen'. I tend to agree with MacGillivray rather than Keith, for this mountain has always been the mountain of my heart, and will hopefully be that of my ashes.

The ascent of Beinn a' Bhuird by Victoria took place in a much more placid political climate than that of Lochnagar in 1848. By 1850 the revolutionary wave in Europe had passed, with order everywhere restored. The German states, including Albert's Saxe-Coburg, were once again under Austrian domination. Victoria had visited Dublin in August 1849, where she had been pleased with her welcome. 'It was a wonderful and striking scene,' she wrote, 'when one reflects how lately the country had been in open revolt and under martial law'. In Britain the Chartist menace had evaporated in the new prosperity, soon to be symbolised by the Great Exhibition of 1851 – opened by Vikki and Albert themselves.

Victoria could not see Beinn a' Bhuird from Balmoral, but she had seen and admired it from the ascent of Lochnagar, and a little less than two years afterwards she added the Table Mountain to her bag of hills. This time she took a route which corresponds much more to that taken today by walkers and climbers, than that followed by her on Lochnagar. The royal party drove from Balmoral past Invercauld House to somewhere in the vicinity of the present Alltdourie cottage, where they found their ponies (Vikki's appropriately named Lochnagar) and people. They walked a little way, then mounted their ponies to ascend Gleann a-t Slugain (the *Sluggan*), which Victoria had been informed means 'swallowing', though 'throat' is a more usual explanation, from its obvious shape. At this point she observed 'There is an excellent path, almost a narrow road, made up to within the last two miles' – which is still the case, until the glen narrows further. Half way to their mountain the party observed 'a very pretty little shooting box, called *Sluggan Cottage*, which is half way from *Invercauld* to the top of *Ben-na-Bourd*'. Some of the stone, timber and slates from the ruins of Slugain Cottage was used in the 1950s by Aberdonian climbers to make a pair of secret howffs nearby, giving shelter and security from prying gamekeepers on the estate. They are still in use, but not easily found. These howffs were and are used by climbers such as Freddy Malcolm who developed Coire na Ciche on Beinn a' Bhuird in the '50s. Again, as with Lochnagar, on the Table Mountain – with notable exceptions like the Crofton-Cumming Route – little climbing had been done before 1945. In the glen they were also shown a stone supposedly remaining from the house of Finla, founder of the Farquharsons.

Once into open country, they forded the Quoich and headed for Carn Fiaclach, 'Tooth's Craig' according to Victoria's informants, where the ground steepened and the path disintegrated, '...very stony; in fact, nothing but bare granite'. This forced them to alternately walk and ride, until they came to the 'perfectly flat' top, and crossed to the main summit at 3,940ft according to Vikki, who was still using Keith's measurements, the OS maps of the area not yet having been published. Then 'We sat down at a cairn and had our luncheon' – admiring the view on a 'very hot' day. Unlike on Lochnagar, they had a clear view in all directions from the summit, even seeing ships on the Moray Firth through a telescope. The day was enlivened by the finding of Cairngorm

## WALK 9: BEINN A' BHUIRD (Map F)
### 18 miles, 7½ – 9 hours

*Following in Victoria's tracks today, you cannot start at Alltdourie, as this is on a private Invercauld estate road, but must begin a mile and a half further down, leaving a car, if you have one, just off the road and passing the hamlet of Keiloch. Approaching Alltdourie are signs directing you away from the cottage. The Scottish Rights of Way Society recently co-operated with the estate in re-routing the traditional path to preserve the privacy of this estate cottage, a course of action the SRWS seem to have limitless enthusiasm for. Thereafter the route is very obvious as far as Slugain Cottage (Vikki's 'pretty little shooting-box') which is now very ruinous. It is possible thereafter to follow Victoria's route up past Carn Fiaclach, as long as the Quoich is not in spate. But most walkers head northwards for Clach a' Chleirich, along a good, well-trodden path, and then directly to the north top, as this allows the panorama of the corries of Beinn a' Bhuird to unfold majestically as you walk. A circular route, crossing from the north to the south top and descending by Victoria's route of ascent, is the best option. (OS 36 and 43)*

stones, both on the summit and by Albert walking in Gleann a-t Slugain. 'It had been a delightful expedition,' records Vikki, also mentioning that for her Lochnagar was still 'the jewel of all the mountains here'.

On descent you will undoubtedly see the scars of a horrendous track, bulldozed from the Mar Estate virtually to the top of Beinn a' Bhuird, the relic of a failed ski experiment in the '60s. I have encountered a Land Rover on the top of Beinn a' Bhuird, driven up this horrible scar. Thankfully, acquisition of the Mar Estate by the National Trust for Scotland has led to the initiation of a plan to remove the scar, over time; in the meantime, nothing stops other lairds bulldozing tracks into the heart of our hills. The reconciliation of sporting landlordism with the public interest remains as problematic as ever.

# The Hill of the Black Pig: Ben MacDhui

From the summit of Beinn a' Bhuird Victoria recorded that she could see Ben MacDhui in the Duke of Fife's forest, yet it was almost ten years before she trod the summit of the highest of the Cairngorm hills. That decade was one of unprecedented economic expansion and prosperity for Britain – now recognised as the Workshop of the World – and of social peace. It was also one of increasing popularity for the monarchy, with Albert patronising artistic and scientific endeavours, despite his hypochondria.

Whether it be named after the progeny of Duff, or in honour of the black pig (boar) which used to roam its slopes, MacDhui and all the Mar Forest had come into the possession of the Duffs, later Dukes of Fife, subsequent to the forfeitures following the Jacobite Rebellions of the 18th century. Long the haunt of bandits, poachers and distillers, the forest was gradually brought some-what within the rule of law by soldiers posted at various points, including Braemar itself, who patrolled the area, after the '45. The OS men had been out mapping the mountain in the 1840s, and the ruins of some of their constructions can still be seen on Ben MacDhui's summit. The mountain had been climbed before this, by the ubiquitous Rev Keith, who had ascended and measured it in 1810, and to the consternation of local people, proved it was lower than Ben Nevis; previously it was widely assumed to be the highest mountain in Britain. Some local patriots persisted in their refusal to budge, like the Rev Anderson, Vikki's minister, who claimed in 1842 in the OSA that,

'According to the last geometrical survey by order of the Government, this mountain (Ben MacDhui) was found to be 20 feet higher than Ben Nevis, which was beforehand considered to be the highest in Britain.'

The royal party trundled out the sociable and drove to Castleton, still the generally used name for Braemar at that time, and then took post horses to the Shiel of the Derry ('that beautiful spot'), where the ponies and luncheon baskets were waiting. This shiel was in the vicinity of the present Derry Lodge, but that building was only constructed later. They were led up Glen Derry by George McHardy, 'an elderly man who knew the country (and acts as a guide, carrying luggage across the hills 'on beasts' which he keeps for that purpose)'. Glen Derry Victoria thought very fine, observing 'the remnants of a splendid forest'. The Muckle Spate of 1829 and commercial felling had already much reduced this forest from the time, over two centuries before, when John Taylor had observed that the Earl of Mar 'hath as many firre-trees growing there as would serve for masts (from this time to the end of the worlde) for all the shippes... that are now or can be in the worlde'. The path up the Derry Vikki says was very bad, and 'broken up by the cattle coming down for the 'Tryst' ', which is a reminder that at this time the path they were on, the Lairig an Laoigh, was still in use to drive the calves to market in Crieff and Falkirk from the West Highlands, as the Lairig Ghru was too difficult for the young cattle.

The ascent of MacDhui was made by turning into Corrie Etchachan, or *Corrie Etchan* in Victoria's account, and entering 'a very wild rugged spot, with magnificent precipices' as indeed they are, Corrie Etchachan being today one of the best rock climbing areas in the Cairngorms. Passing *Ben Main* [Beinn Mheadhoin] on the right – which was incidentally my own last Munro – they came up by a 'very steep ascent' to Loch Etchachan where the mist came down and they proceeded in the 'piercing cold wind' to the summit for lunch. The ascent, partly riding, partly walking, had taken just over three hours. On the summit they had good luck and the mist cleared 'and exhibited the grandest, wildest scenery imaginable!' – giving them views to Beinn a' Bhuird, Beinn a' Ghloe and the Wells of Dee. Victoria comments that '*Ben Muich Dhui* is 4,297 feet high, one of the highest mountains *in Scotland*' – which is at least diplomatic, on its relationship to Nevis.

They picnicked on top, ran about looking for Cairngorm stones, and Victoria adds, 'I had a little whisky and water, as the people declared pure water would be too chilling'. Victoria's good spirits on the mountains – John Brown commented to her on the ascent of MacDhui that it was a pleasure to walk with someone who was 'always content' – were partly achieved by ingestion of quantities of 'the water of life', to which she was very partial, adding it to her tea as well as to her water. Brown figures prominently in this ascent of MacDhui, 'my pony being led by Brown most of the time going up and down', Victoria comments. The servant had developed a style of attendance on the monarch, a certain iconoclastic sycophancy, which, with the whisky, boosted Victoria's feel-good factor. Brown told her, for example, that of Albert 'Every one on the estate says there was never so kind a master. I am sure our only wish is to give satisfaction.' Possibly thinking her readers might find Brown over-familiar, when the account of this ascent was published in 1868, Victoria added a footnote explaining that 'We were always in the habit of conversing with the Highlanders – with whom one comes so much in contact in the Highlands... [their] good breeding, simplicity and intelligence... make it so pleasant and even instructive to talk to them.' Like so much gracious condescension of that period, such comments the modern reader finds rather patronising.

The day on the mountain, 7 October 1859, had gone well, and Victoria said of it, 'Never shall I forget this day, or the impression this very grand scene made upon me; truly sublime and impressive; such solitude.'

The estate remained in the hands of the Duke of Fife for many years after Victoria's ascent of MacDhui. As deer stalking became more and more lucrative, a real infrastructure was developed; Derry Lodge was built, and also Corrour Bothy as a watchers' house deep in the Lairig Ghru, in 1875. As the old droving trade declined, the Duke tried to prevent the new interloper, the walker and climber, disturbing the deer. Walkers were obstructed by Fife's gamekeepers, leading to one walker writing in 1878 and denouncing as intolerable 'Our native Mumbo Jumbos who molest the traveller in Glen Derry, Glen Lui Beg and other wilds' – a specific reference to the Mar estate, which called for walkers to ignore all attempts to prevent access. And like the Queen's, Fife's tenants were forbidden giving accommodation to outsiders. Eventually, though, Maggie Gruer at Inverey won this right for the Duke's tenants after World War One, by a campaign of letter writing to the press. Maggie was a redoubtable soul; on one occasion she proudly announced she had 'fuppit the royal dug' for annoying her cows. A dedicated anti-Tory, Maggie recalled the Liberal leader Gladstone visiting her parents at Thistle Cottage when she herself was a girl.

But despite this policy of obstruction, the mountain became increasingly popular to climb, one of its ascenders being the Liberal Prime Minister himself, when visiting Victoria at Balmoral, in a round trip of 25 miles. In 1887, the year of Victoria's Jubilee, there was an especially important ascent of the mountain. Some Aberdeen walkers climbed MacDhui on 22 June to add a firework display to the general celebratory countrywide illuminations. 'Around us on all sides... the country was lit up with blazing bonfires... we unpacked our cases and added to the general enlightenment by a continuous discharge of rockets and other fireworks...'. The party descended to the Shelter Stone, and the next day agreed to found the Cairngorm Club, one of the earliest of Scottish mountaineering organisations.

But not all celebrations of the Jubilee went as well. In November an assembly for Free Speech in Trafalgar Square, which took the form of a 'mock' celebration of Victoria's half century on the throne, organised by socialists and the unemployed, turned into the severest rioting and violence seen in the capital for decades, known as Bloody Sunday. A mock speech from the throne, part drafted by Bernard Shaw, commented that, 'the vast wealth produced by the labour of my people, is now not only distributed not only unequally but also inequably...'. It is possibly a significant indicator of the decline of monarchist sentiment that the mountaineering community did not celebrate the Jubilee of Elizabeth in 1977 in the same way as that of her predecessor. (Though the Scottish Mountaineering Club was still, as late as 1991 at a dinner I attended, proposing the Loyal Toast!) And just as Victoria's Jubilee was marred by the Trafalgar Square Riots, so the fairytale marriage of the 20th century between Prince Charming and Snow White in 1981 had as its mocking counterpart the inner city rioting marked by levels of violence new in Britain. History has a way of arranging its ironies.

And MacDhui itself? After the Duffs sold the estate it went through the hands of various owners in a gradually downward spiral of neglect and environmental decay. One owner tried misconceived plans at ski-ing. Another, the American Kluge, bought it so his wife could bide beside the Queen, and so on.... It was recently acquired by the National Trust for Scotland, which has various exciting plans for the estate, including the reduction of deer numbers which had undergone a huge explosion, and restoration of tree cover – one day the Derry forest may be restored to something like what Taylor saw in 1618. As MacDhui is on National Trust land, there are no access problems or difficulties. You can follow the road up to Derry Lodge, observing on your left the extensive remains of villages cleared in the 18th century. Lord

---

### WALK 10: BEN MacDHUI (Map F)
### 20 miles (from Linn o Dee), 8 – 11 hours

*At the ruins of Derry Lodge do not take the eyesore of a bull-dozed track up the east of the glen, which is scheduled for removal, but follow the old drove road and Victoria's route, through the pine woods on the west bank of the river, and thence traverse the glen where path restoration and tree conservation is in evidence. Elsewhere on the estate there are plans to restore river wetlands as breeding habitats for birds, an extensive programme of path maintenance is being undertaken, and last but far from least, archeological surveys on the remains of the buildings used by those who once lived here are being done. Rising past the Etchachan Hut (a base for those climbing on the surrounding rocks), the route to the summit taken by Victoria is tracked and easy to follow, past Loch Etchachan and the ruins of the Trigonometers near the summit. From that summit marvel and reflect that the localised euthenasia of private landlordism in the Mar Forest means that this landscape will be forever preserved, and improved, for your benefit. (Though not everyone is happy, as voluntary restrictions on mountain biking on the estate are being sought.) (OS 43 and a tiny bit of 36)*

Grange, brother of the forfeit Earl of Mar, wrote in 1726 telling his factor to 'eject these people after their harvest is over... the more [men] you have with you there will be the less opposition... [in order] that people may see they they are not to be suffered in their illegal insolence.' And yet writers who should know better say there were few evictions on Deeside.

Victoria now had four mountains over 3,000ft to her credit. To my knowledge, at that time (1859) there were probably only about a dozen people – scientists, mapmakers and odd eccentrics – who had climbed any more of Scotland's peaks. But she was not finished yet, and would further add to her tally.

**A Highland piper (c1850) by Gavarni.**
(Aberdeen Art Gallery and Museums)
A piper with an admiring audience, including a wee boy who has lost interest in his toy to the music. Gavarni's tartan clad, cherubic peasants are imaginary people, in an idealised location. The attempt to outlaw Highland dress, tartan and the pipes after the '45 was one of the most ineffective measures on statute, and was soon abandoned. But it was the Highlanders' participation in the wars of the British Empire that turned the rebel into a hero. Victoria appears to have enjoyed the skirl of the pipes, though many of her guests did not.

**Schiehallion and Tummel Bridge (1802) by Sir Thomas Dick Lauder**
(Aberdeen Art Gallery and Museums)

The road shown is one constructed by General Wade, from Aberfeldy to Rannoch, where there was a barracks in the pacification period. After the '45 General Roy was engaged in mapping the Highlands for the British Army, especially the roads and the mountains, including the area around Schiehallon. He returned in 1774 to visit the mountain when the astronomer Nevil Maskelyne was conducting experiments on it, to determine the density of the earth. On the visit Roy climbed the mountain and measured its height barometrically. On her 1866 tour of Perthshire, when she took this road, Victoria noted 'Schiehallion, one of the high hills.'

### The Shelter Stone at Loch Avon (1816) by Sir Thomas Dick Lauder
(Aberdeen Art Gallery and Museums)

A desperately remote spot in pre-chairlift days. The figures have the usual 'Celtic' touches in their dress. The Shelter Stone (Clach Dion) has an interesting history. It was reputedly used by the notorious Wolf of Badenoch in the 14th century, and later was a hideaway for a gang of robbers. In 1887, Clach Dion provided sleeping quarters for a group of Aberdeen walkers who had just celebrated Victoria's Jubilee by a fireworks display on Ben MacDhui; on waking, they decided to form the Cairngorm Club. Victoria visited Loch Avon in 1861, observing that 'nothing could be grander and wilder', but did not reach the Shelter Stone.

**Putting the Stone (c1850) by Michel Bouquet**
(Aberdeen Art Gallery and Museums)

Thirled to the picturesque/romantic view of life in the hills, Bouquet here gives us a fine strapping, healthy laddie, in Highland dress, putting the stone to admiring glances. In fairness, however, putting the stone was an authentic and traditional Highland game. The nineteenth century Highland games movement, with its invented dress codes and competitions of dubious heritage, spread rapidly once legitimised by Victoria. Indeed, many Lowland towns took up the habit, and celebrated, in an invented form, the Celtic civilisation which had been destroyed by the advance of Lowland culture.

**Balmoral Castle (1849) by Michel Bouquet**
(Aberdeen Art Gallery and Museums)

The residence of Victoria and Albert brought prosperity to Upper Deeside, but the blessings were not unmixed. Tenants on the estate were forbidden to have lodgers or take in guests, to preserve royal privacy. Royal residence had its impact on transport too, and a right of way which passed the castle was re-routed by Act of Parliament. This had not yet happened, and here it looks as if the cattle are about to cross the ford to the old road on the far side. Bouquet adds the obligatory tartan clad piper to complete the scene. But it is highly unlikely that a cattleman would have driven his beasts playing the pipes. This is a composition, in the literal sense.

**Highlanders' Huts (1849) by Michel Bouquet**
(Aberdeen Art Gallery and Museums)

A soft focus on thatched Highland houses, though Bouquet does style them 'huts'. Although they could be treated thus romantically in a sylvan setting, most observers in the 1840s, years of widespread want in the Highlands, commented on the poor quality of the local housing. Victoria, travelling from Fort William to Glencoe observed 'The cottages along the roadside here and there hardly deserve the name, and are indeed mere hovels (except for) some very ragged dirty old people, and very scantily clothed, dishevelled children, you would not believe they were meant for human habitation'. But such a reality was not one the Victorian middle classes wished to hang above their mantelpieces, and the market for works such as Bouquet's was enormous.

**Stream in the Highlands (1848) by Michel Bouquet**
(Aberdeen Art Gallery and Museums)

Another picturesque Bouquet scene; what could be more uplifting than a Highland shepherd tending his flock in Arcadian surroundings? However, where sheep were introduced, most infamously in the Sutherland Clearances, the result was an expulsion of the indigenous population, and a much longer-term degradation of the environment. It was an imagined reality, and imagined Highlanders, that artists presented to their public at this period.

**Girls Washing Clothes (c1850) by Gavarni**
(Aberdeen Art Gallery and Museums)
In an idealised, romanticised Highlands, we have idealised, romanticised Highlanders. Here we find very
well-groomed and well-fed Highland lassies, who look more like the damsels of a pre-Raphaelite painting
than Highland peasants. And as always, the tartan touch is in evidence. The later development of
photography in the works of such as Washington Wilson, which showed Highland poverty, helped dispel the
Romanticised image of life in the mountains. Vikki liked to watch the 'rosie-faced lassies' at work, but she
would have probably found too much leg on display here.

# CHAPTER 4

# The Big Trips

THERE ARE MANY WHO, despite the current mania for day-out mountaineering, feel that only overnighters are real mountain men – or women. Victoria clearly shared this view, and increasing frustration at returning home after a day on the hills led to a series of overnight 'Expeditions' as she called them. Though hardly sleeping under stones while away from Balmoral, these trips showed Vikki was a game lass nonetheless. Victoria describes the usually effortless precision of her trips, but we should remember that behind every outing with a few loyal gillies, massive preparations had been made by hordes of domestics. Cooks and maids had packed food and clothing, grooms had prepared horses, and ponies were organised and waiting at strategic points. Hoteliers and even policemen had been forewarned as to royal progress, as had landowners en route, all these tasks being carried out by armies of retainers. One wonders if Victoria ever thought about this, or just imagined that all this neo-feudal dependency was just 'how it was'. Certainly the myth of Vikki liking the 'simple life' needs to be exploded. On one trip to Cliveden, for example, Victoria took a staff of 91, including *three* doctors. Most of the British population at that time would have had difficulty in gaining access to one.

## By Feshie and Tamintowl

On 4 September 1860 the royal party went in the sociable to Braemar, where they changed horses and advanced to the Shepherd's Shiel of Geldie, and there the ponies and a guide, Charlie Stewart, awaited. Victoria says nothing about her journey till she came to the vicinity of the Geldie, where she describes the scenery hitherto as 'wild... bare of trees... and not picturesque'.

But her route along Glen Dee past Inverey and the Linn o Dee is one rich in associations. Inverey itself was a community of over one hundred souls at this time, many of them recently evicted from Glen Ey by the Duke of Fife to create a deer forest; the ruins of their settlements are still visible half way up the glen. The village was also the birthplace of John Lamont, born in 1805, who later became Professor of Astronomy at Munich, and ultimately the Astronomer-Royal of Bavaria. There is a memorial to him in the village, unveiled in 1934 with Maggie Gruer (a distant relative) present.

At the Linn o Dee Victoria would have crossed the present stone bridge, built in 1857 and opened by herself, and celebrated with a good dram of whisky, then headed up Glen Dee. Here again she was amongst ruins, whose inhabitants had departed or been cleared from villages like *Dubrach*, near the Chest o Dee, though the royal eye may not have been able to translate the rickles of drystane dykes into former habitations, for she says nothing about them. The 1:25,000 map shows them: *Dalvorar, Tonnagaoithe, Tomnamoine.*

*Dubrach* was the birthplace of Patrick Grant, the last Jacobite survivor of Culloden, who died in 1824 and was buried in Braemar, after a Jacobite funeral. Patrick was introduced to Victoria's for-bear George IV by Walter Scott four years before his death as 'Your Majesty's Oldest Friend'. Grant took the liberty of correcting Wattie as follows: 'Na, na, I'm His Majesty's Auldest Enemy.' Apparently George was not amused, but I am sure Vikki would have been. In 1759 Dubrach was tenanted by a Redcoat outpost, under Sergeant Davies. Davies was out alone one day on a shoulder of Carn Bhac above Glen Ey, and meeting two men armed and in tartan, challenged them. They in turn murdered him, and buried him on the high tops. Tried in 1754 for his murder, both men were surprisingly acquitted.

The scenery began to find more royal approval, being described as 'very fine' once the Geldie area was passed. They came to the *Etchart* [Eidart], 'a very deep ford', where the men waded through after taking shoes and socks off, and 'Grant, on his pony, led me through'. After crossing the watershed at the Eidart the expedition began to descend into Glen Feshie, or *Fishie* as Vikki called it, describing the glen as containing 'some of the most beautiful scenery possible'. After the bleakness of the Geldie, Glen Feshie was a welcome contrast. The 'rapid river is overhung by rocks, with trees, birch and fir... the hills as you advance rise very steeply on both sides, with rocks and corries and occasional streamlets... It is quite magnificent!', she commented, and the party picnicked amongst the splendid native Scots pines by the river. And indeed, it is magnificent.

Victoria may not have known much about art, but she knew what she liked. Apart from having a large collection of nude and semi-nude paintings – at a time when prudery was generally rampant – Vikki liked landscapes, lots of torrents, bens, mist and coos. The artist Edwin Landseer was one of her favourite painters, indeed he painted Victoria at Loch Laggan, in a typical idyllic Highland landscape. She had his engravings photographed and bound for her after his death. Landseer had visted Feshie several times, and stayed at an 'encampment', today marked on the map as Ruigh-aiteachain, built by the Duchess of Bedford. Victoria passed this 'scene of all Landseer's glory', commenting sadly on 'the wooden and turf huts... all falling into decay'. The scene today is still marked by a standing lum. Indeed, almost a century after this royal visit the frescoes were still visible – though now, alas, gone.

Met by Lord and Lady Russell, Victoria and Albert were escorted out of the glen, being shown the tourist sites as they went, the monument to the Duke of Gordon on one hilltop, the Argyll Stone on another, the latter ironically a spot where the Marquis of Argyll stopped during the Covenanting wars, on a trip to punish the 'Popish' Gordons. Afterwards the party descended to Loch Insch, 'which is lovely', and crossed the Spey by a ferry, before driving by road to Grantown, where they spent the night. The drive was in 'two shabby vehicles' pulled by 'rather miserable horses', but Victoria didn't mind, she was enjoying the adventure and the view towards the Cairngorm mountains. After dinner she wrote up her log, while Albert played patience. Victoria liked her grub, and tucked into 'soup, 'hodge-podge', mutton broth with vegetables... fowl with white sauce, good roast lamb, very good potatoes, besides one or two other dishes... ending with a good tart of cranberries'. And so to bed, where I'm sure she lay back and thought of Scotland.

Next day, despite their travelling incognito (or rather as Lord and Lady Churchill) and without pomp and circumstance, the royal couple were discovered and treated to an outbreak of monarchical fervour, as Grantown went wild. Or moderately so – their landlady waved a handkerchief, and a maid waved a flag. Their route back to Balmoral took Victoria and Albert by road again, as far as Tomintoul, by Daldhu and the *Bridge of Bruin* [Brig o Broon] and the *Bridge of Avon*. Tomintoul did not impress Victoria. Despite her desire to see everything in the Highlands through romantic spectacles, the reality of Highland poverty could not altogether escape her.

'Tomintoul is the most tumble-down, poor-looking place I ever saw – a long street with three inns, miserable dirty looking houses and people, and a sad look of wretchedness about it. Grant told me that it was the dirtiest, poorest village in the whole Highlands.'

From Tomintoul they headed southwards up Glen Avon, and lunched, before continuing to Inchrory, where 'Brown and two of the others walked before us at a fearful pace', and where they had been the year previously. They were delighted by the sight of a pair of eagles, one of Victoria's few fauna or flora comments. On again to Loch Builg, 'beautifully lit up by the setting sun'. Here carriages were waiting, and they drove down the Gairn and then back to Balmoral, where she penned her next *Journal* entry on 'this very amusing and never to be forgotten expedition, which will always be remembered with delight'. However, Victoria feels obliged, yet again, to unaccountably give praise to Albert: 'To my dear Albert we owe it...' – though not quite all. John Brown's doglike devotion had already impressed the Queen, and she comments favourably on Grant and Brown, 'the latter, particularly, is handy and willing to do everything, and to overcome any difficulty, which makes him one of my best servants anywhere.' The pony, Fyvie, also gets a journalistic pat on the back.

Victoria had passed through familiar country that day, especially in Glen Gairn, where she had been a few times. But did she *know* it? I doubt not, and here is the reason why. She was fascinated by *Rob Roy*, referring to that novel more than any other work of Scott. But Rob had been on her doorstep! Glen Gairn had been an area to which MacGregors were exiled in the 17th century, changing their names to Grier, Griesk, Gruer... and Gregory. Rob Roy himself had actually visited Glen Gairn prior to the 1715 Rising, attempting to raise his kinsmen for the Stuarts, and in this he experienced success. Less success was had when he visited another kinsman in Aberdeen, Dr Gregory, Professor of Mathematics, and tried to enlist his support also. While haranguing the reluctant academic, Rob heard the sound of soldiers, and fled the city, 'louping the Leuchar burn' at Culter on his way back up Deeside. A statue now stands at the spot. One only knows a landscape when one knows it historically and socially, and this Vikki never did, could never do.

Following in Victoria's footsteps on this expedition poses problems for those without horses and carriages, and a large retinue of servants to deal with the logistical problems. A compliant life partner and a car would be of advantage.

Had things proved otherwise, a bridge might have been built over the Eidart much earlier. After the 1715 Rebellion, which started on Deeside, General Wade planned to build a military road from Braemar Castle to Ruthven barracks on the Spey; the area was surveyed, Wade drew up maps, estimated the siting of important bridges and costed the construction at £3,200. The road was never built, but even in the 1960s plans were afoot to connect Aberdeen with the growing holiday resort of Aviemore by such a road. Now there is thankfully no chance it will ever be constructed.

On the Feshie side, we come across a stark contrast to that obtaining in Mar. A succession of private owners, with generous access to the public purse, has wrought havoc here. The Scots Pine and juniper which Victoria admired are ageing and in bad condition,

## WALK 11: THROUGH FESHIE (Map F)
### 22 miles, 8 – 12 hours

*From the Linn o Dee a land-rover track goes as far as White Bridge; en route you will hopefully have a look at some of the ruined buildings and lime kilns. The vehicle track continues beyond this to Ruigh nan Clach (a serviceable bothy I howffed in thirty years ago, now ruinous) and then Geldie Lodge, which is also a ruin, like the other shepherds' and gamekeepers' cottages which replaced the clachans of those evicted. The Mar Estate, of which Glen Dee here is part, is now owned by the National Trust. As well as massively culling deer numbers to encourage natural tree regeneration, the Trust is also pursuing a policy of removing many of the bulldozed tracks on the estate; it is likely that in time White Bridge will be the limit of such man-make tracks, and the going thereafter less easy. On the opposite bank to the ruins of the Lodge at the Geldie runs a goodish path goes over the watershed to Glen Feshie; at the Eidart there is now a bridge some little distance upsteam from the ancient ford. An ill-maintained bulldozed track, suffering from landslide erosion, takes you into the flats of Feshie and past the lum which is all that is left of Landseer's bothy, although a byre nearby has been restored as a mountain bothy and offers shelter in bad weather. At a bridge further on, you cross to the west bank of the river and meet with a tarred estate road, which takes you southwards and out of the glen. Hopefully your life partner is as reliable as Brown, and waiting at Achlean, the end of the public road, reached by crossing back to the right bank of the river. This is a long walk, and the return journey will probably take another day, with an overnight on Speyside. (OS 43)*

or fenced in unsightly and damaging enclosures. Deer numbers are out of control, and that in a region where the first gamekeeper, Collie, in the 1840s had to poach deer from neighbouring estates to start a deer forest! Not everyone shared landlord enthusiasm about the creation of such 'forests'. Here are the words of one Victorian commentator, whom one might have thought would have had other things on his mind.

'Scotland is the last refuge of the 'noble passion'... The deer forests of Scotland contain not a single tree. The sheep are driven from, and the deer driven to, the naked hills and then it is called a deer forest. Not even timber-planting and real forest culture.' (*Capital*, Vol.1, Karl Marx.)

## WALK 12: TOMINTOUL TO GLENGAIRN (Map F)
### 18 miles, 7 – 10 hours

*The walk to Inchrory from Tomintoul starts a little south of the village at the appropriately named 'Queen's View', and is on a good estate road after the public road ends at a locked gate a couple of miles in. Then a delightful ascent through juniper and birch woods brings you to Inchrory, a distance before which the tarred road becomes dirt track. Thereafter all but a short section up beside Loch Builg is on land-rover tracks; easy walking, but hard on the limbs. On the route back to the public road, pause at the ruins of Corndavon Lodge, an architectural paradigm of Victorian class society: the muckle hoose for the laird (Invercauld land here) and his guests or leasees, and on the other side of the burn the various buildings of the servant class, the stables for the horses, and the butchering huts for the dead deer – all the smelly bits! These outbuildings once housed a bothy, restored by hillwalkers, but it was closed by the Invercauld estate a while back. The best way to finish this walk is to continue down the Gairn and come out at Gairnshiel bridge, the magnificent Caulfeild construction on the Military Road. It would be nice to have a sociable or a barouche waiting, but you will probably be glad enough to see a motor car. (OS 36 and 37)*

In the late 19th century the Catholic priest of Glengairn, Father Thomas Meany, took down tales and lore from the declining, though still vibrant, community of Gairnside; the manuscript, in broad Doric Scots, is discussed in Robert Smith's wonderful little book, *Land of the Lost*, which explores the vanished communities of Deeside. The ruins you will have walked through if you do this walk were once farms, inns, shops, mills; indeed one *clachan* was nicknamed 'The Metropoleon' because 'fowk had a'thing amang themselves'. I will borrow no more: read Smith's book.

## *At Feshie again – and full Tilt*

Victoria went on another trip through Feshie the following year, and we can conveniently deal with it coupled with its partner. On a threatening day, 8 October 1861, she and her man, with their men, again reached the Geldie, where the same guide as last year, Stewart, waited. High waters forced them to ford frequently as they progressed. It was raining heavily, and Vikki was happit up in a plaid, with an umbrella to shelter her from the elements, a sight worth seeing, I'm sure. Brown had the job of leading Vikki's pony – Inchrory – through the Eidart, where a bundle of cloaks fell in the water. But the weather cleared as they entered the Feshie, where, joined by General Grey, they 'lunched hurriedly' before proceeding along a 'path so narrow as to make it utterly unsafe to ride', and arriving again at Ruigh-aiteachain.

This time Victoria had clearly been informed about the Landseer frescoes, and when they came to the encampment, they halted to investigate.

'The huts, surrounded by magnificent fir-trees, and by quantities of juniper bushes, looked lovelier than ever; and we gazed with sorrow at their utter ruin... We got off and went into one of the huts to look at a fresco of stags of Landseer's, over a chimney-piece.'

On leaving Glen Feshie the carriages were waiting, and they drove 29 miles to Dalwhinnie, via Kingussie, 'a very straggling place'. She mentions seeing the 'ruined castle of Ruthven', which was actually the Hanoverian military barracks built after the 1715, and extended by Wade in 1734, though no one appeared able to tell her that. At this time the road through Drumochter was still the main route from Perth to Inverness, and a two or three day journey. It had originally been constructed by General Wade, and was ironically used for the passage south of the Jacobite army in 1745. A week after Victoria's trip the first sod was cut in James Mitchell's Highland Railway, and by 1863 the Inverness to Perth journey would take little more than three hours. As well as revolutionising transport, the railway would have other far-reaching effects. On the following day, after leaving Dalwhinnie, Victoria observed that, 'We passed many drovers, without their herds and flocks, returning, Grant told us, from Falkirk.' Already in decline, droving would be killed by the railways.

And Vikki was not sad to leave Dalwhinnie, for although the accommodation in the hotel was spacious,

'... there was hardly anything to eat, and there was only tea, and two miserable starved Highland chickens, without any potatoes! No pudding, and no *fun*... ...Grant, Brown and Stewart... had only the remains of our two starved chickens.'

I am sure she would have enjoyed much more the conviviality of the present Dalwhinnie Transport Café, last refuge of climbers, lorry drivers and locals, where there is plenty of food and lots of fun. However, even that establishment could not supply the entertainment that awaited Victoria in the morning. Cluny MacPherson, holding no grudge that she did not buy land at Loch Laggan, had arrived with his pipers and Volunteers, who presented a military guard for Victoria as she set off over the Drumochter Pass.

Although in certain metallic lights, or on a white winter's day, Drumochter has a grandeur, the journey is not the favourite of many people. The German novelist and tourist Fontane, who had come that way in 1859, had described it as the most desolate landscape he had ever seen. But Victoria was always positive, and according to her the pass contained 'Fine and very wild scenery, high wild hills... ...a little further on we came to Loch Garry, which is very beautiful.' As they descended the Garry, they were met by the Duke of Atholl, and soon the royal couple were in sight of country they knew: 'it cleared when we came in sight of *Ben-y-Ghlo*.' For they had been here all of seventeen years before, when Victoria had done her first Munro.

The party were conducted by Bruar falls, where they had walked in 1844, though time permitted no stop; it did permit Victoria, however, to regret that the proposed railway would pass by the falls, and disturb its peace. It had taken about three hours to come from Dalwhinnie to Blair Castle, indicating a speed of less than ten miles an hour on such a road as was the old military causeway. After a quick cup of coffee with the Duchess and a chat over old times, they were away again – on a boat! Victoria tells that they 'then got into the carriage, a very peculiar one, viz, a *boat*, – a mere boat (which is very light), put on four wheels, drawn by a pair of horses with a postilion.' She says the servants found it 'a great treat', and I'm sure Vikki did too.

Since Victoria had last passed this way, a celebrated conflict had taken place which laid open Glen Tilt to public access. In 1847 a party of Edinburgh botanists was passing through the Glen en route to the Cairngorm area when they were confronted and harassed by the Duke's gamekeepers. The Duke himself spurred on his keepers, destroying a bridge to limit access and assaulting the Provost of Perth, whose Town Council backed the access fight. The fight had been won by the time of Victoria's return in 1861, though it is doubtful that she knew anything about such events. Nor did she appear to know that 'poor Queen Mary', whose fate she was always lamenting, had been here three centuries before her. At a great hunting party in 1563, some 2,000 men had worked for weeks to ensure that a similar number of deer would be available for a successful drive. In those days, deer were driven to enclosures, designated as *elrig* on old maps, and pulled down by gun, arrow and hounds. On this occasion 360 deer were killed, as well as five wolves... and a number of the deer drivers, trampled to death when the herd ran over them. Mary was reported as being 'delighted with the sport'.

Atholl's argument for attempting to prevent access in the 1840s had been that a few botanists would do irreparable damage to his deer forest. However, his reception for Victoria, in the middle of the shooting season, showed these were simply hollow excuses to keep his domain private. Beasts terrified by botanists, according to the Chookie, would apparently be unperturbed by Victoria's large entourage proceeding up the glen, preceded by a pair of pipers, and meeting all her old pals from 1844 as they went! Peter Frazer (so-spellt by Vikki this time) and Sandy McAra, now head-keeper, were encountered as they went up the glen towards Forest Lodge, and Vikki was genuinely glad to see them. Here the cast of dozens which backed up Victoria's trips again becomes clear. Their ponies had been brought from Balmoral, after having spent the night at the *Bainoch or Beynoch* [Bynack Shiel].

Led by Sandy and still accompanied by the Duke, the party proceeded up the Tilt by the old drove road to a luncheon spot, roughly opposite where the Tilt is joined by the Allt Lochain burn. It is an indication of how a person like Victoria, not devoid of humanity, could accept the presumptions of Victorian class society. They sketched, they lunched and afterwards she commented, 'the remainder was as usual given to the men...' – almost as if they were loyal dogs. Indeed, when Vikki praised servants, it was usually in the terminology one would apply to animals: faithful, devoted, obedient and so forth. After luncheon came the high point of the trip, the crossing of the Poll Tarf.

The Tarf burn comes down to the Tilt from wild mountain country and can carry much water. Where the rivers join, there is a rocky chasm and a deep pool, below the fine and dramatic Falls of Tarf. It is a spot delightful beyond most. Now there is a bridge, the Bedford Memorial built in 1886 by the Rights of Way Society after an English hiker was drowned at this spot, but in Victoria's time fording was the only way across. (A stone bridge had been built here in 1770, but it was deliberately demolished by the estate in 1819 to discourage access through the glen.) What a wonderful sight it must have been to have seen the drovers forcing their beasts across the Poll Tarf. But Vikki's party crossing too was quite a sight, as immortalised by the painter, Carl Haag.

Old Sandy McAra is seen boldly striding forth with his crook, followed by the two pipers playing all the time, though the water came up to their waists, and the current was strong. Victoria is following, her pony being led by Brown, whose guidance she preferred to the offer of help from the Duke himself. How that must have flattered Brown's already considerably inflated ego. Soon the party were all across without mishap, either riding or wading. This incident, and its immortalisation by Haag, epitomises more than most the feudal romanticism of Balmorality. We could be in the Middle Ages rather than the Workshop of the World.

Thereafter the path became rougher, and the party struggled across the summit of the pass, sometimes riding but more often being forced to walk. At the county march the Duke gave Victoria and Albert a dram from his hip-flask (such Vikki was never one to refuse), and to the cheers of the men of Atholl, they proceeded to the Bynack, with pipes blaring. With an eye to the picturesque, Vikki comments, 'The ponies went so well with the pipes...'. At Bynack Lady Fife had tea waiting (though I'm sure she did not put a hand to its making herself), and more unseen hands also had the carriages to hand. While the royal pair drove back to Balmoral, the Duke and his servants had to retrace the journey through the mountains in the dark, a hazardous proceeding, Victoria thought, as there was no moon. After dinner Victoria and Albert looked at maps of the Highlands, and she comments in her *Journal* that, 'This was the pleasantest and most enjoyable expedition I ever

## WALK 13: ATHOLL TO MAR (Map G)
### 22 miles, 8½ – 12 hours

*The first part of this walk follows the route given to Carn a' Chlamain, and then continues as far as Forest Lodge. Thence a bulldozed road goes to within a mile or so of the Poll Tarf and the Bedford Bridge, which avoids you having to repeat Victoria's crossing. The track is well worn and easy to follow as far as the watershed, where the narrow Tilt widens to the broad Deeside landscape. Descending from the watershed you come to the ruins of Bynack and thereafter to the crossing of the Geldie Burn, where there is no bridge and difficulties can be encountered if there is a spate. Passing next the forestry plantation surrounding the forlorn remains of Ruigh na Clach, the White Bridge is soon reached, and the track leads thence without complications to the Linn o Dee. Though straitforward, this is a long walk, and rough in parts, and the pedestrian should be well equipped and prepared for bad weather; there are no habitations between Forest Lodge and Linn o Dee. (OS 43)* made; and the recollection of it will always be most agreeable to me, and increase my wish to make more!'

Having described the Feshie walk earlier, the following account will be limited to walking through the Tilt. One of the first people to do so for amusement – not walking but riding through – was Thomas Pennant in 1769. He was not impressed, finding 'the road the most dangerous and the most horrible I have ever travelled', and the Tilt a 'dreary stream'. He encountered people at the shieling, living in turf huts, and subsisting on oatcakes, 'the coagulated blood of their cattle spread on bannocks', and drinking whey and 'sometimes by way of indulgence, whisky'.

## Oer the Hills o Glentanor

There is a wonderful old Scots ballad, in my opinion the greatest of them all, called 'The Baron o Brackley', or sometimes 'Inverey'. In it, Farquharson of Inverey 'came doon Deeside, whistlin and playin', and murdered the Baron o Brackley, in an episode in the longstanding Farquharson-Gordon family feud. Inverey then beds Brackley's wife, and in the morning is given his escape route by her:

> 'Thro Birss and Aboyne', she says, 'lyin in a tour
> Oer the hills o Glentanor ye'll skip in an hour.'

One of Victoria's big expeditions, undertaken just a few weeks before the second Feshie trip, went over much of the ground covered in this ballad, though Albert was not subject to the fate of the poor Baron o Brackley, with Broon in the cuckolding role of Inverey. Victoria seems to have had little knowledge of the history and culture of Upper Deeside such as is described in this ballad. She preferred a simple picture of loyal Highlanders in kilts, engaging in Highland games, and stretching back into the mists of time, in an undifferentiated unity. But then, she was not alone in that, either in her day or in ours. For the record, Inverey, known as the Black Colonel, disappeared after Brackley's murder which occurred in 1666, re-appearing as a colonel in Viscount Dundee's Jacobite Rising of 1689, and being forced once more into hiding, this time in Glen Ey, at a place known as the Colonel's Bed.

Despite Vikki's anxiety at the weather, stout Albert insisted that they set off on 20 September 1861, and as usual is vindicated by the improvement as the mist clears from the hills. They set off in two sociables, 'doon Deeside', though probably not 'whistlin and playin', and changed to ponies at the Bridge of Muick. From here Victoria's directions become a bit vague and confusing. The party crossed the high ground between Glen Muick and Glen Tanar, according to Victoria by a peat road over the hill of *Polach* [Pollagach], where the boggy ground obliged them to dismount, and descended into the *Glen of Corrie Vruach*. Here they were rewarded for their labours with a fine view of Mount Keen, of which she comments:

'Mount Keen is a curious, conical shaped hill, with a deep corrie in it. It is nearly 3,200 feet high, and we had a very steep rough ascent over the shoulder, after crossing the Tanar Water.'

I would think the group crossed into Glen Tanar near the source of the Pollagach Burn by some now vanished peat road, and crossed the Tanar Water somewhere near its head; Vikki mentions the crossing, and says they 'looked down Glen Tanar', so the crossing was high up. Thereupon they picked up the Mounth Road, an old drove road, over Mount Keen's shoulder. Victoria mentions crossing the shoulder of the hill, so it is possible that she may not have added the peak to her bag of Munros, in this way doubtless following the thousands of drovers who had crossed the mountain before her without summitting. But let's be generous, and make up her tally of Munros to five at this point. There is a huge green sward at the foot of the drove road on the Tanar side; this was the drovers' stance, where the animals rested before taking the whole day to cross to Glen Esk, and their manure fertilised the ground. Nearby are ruins, which are those of the old inn of Coirebruach which stood here. The glen itself once supported a fair population. At Etnach, latterly a farm but now deserted, there were once several settlements. Bordland and Braeloyne further down the glen once had 30 people and 17 houses respectively; now the glen is empty.

The first known ascent of Mount Keen has, however, a royal flavour to it. John Taylor, the Water Poet, set out in 1618 on a tour of Scotland, vowing he would rely on native hospitality and not spend any money; his aim was to curry favour with James I and VI, the new Scottish kid on the London royal block. Taylor's *Penyles Pilgrimage* (sic) was a success, and so was the account of it he wrote on returning home. He made money, and friends at Court. He had had adventures too: avoiding the lust of a deaf and dumb wench in Brechin, and staying at 'an Irish house' in Glen Esk where the inhabitants had hardly any English. And he seems to have climbed Mount Keen, for at one point Taylor claims to have been at the top. On the 'exceeding high mountaine called mount Skeene' the Water Poet was caught in a 'Scottish miste' which had his teeth chattering. Victoria had better weather, however, and from Mount Keen's descent, she 'came in sight of a new county, and looked down a very fine glen – Glen Mark.'

The descent was by the Ladder Burn, down 'a very steep but winding path' which was 'very rough' in places to 'a small forester's cottage... a regular Highland cabin, with its usual 'press bed' ' at Invermark, which is Glenmark on the O.S. map, at the junction of the Ladder and Easter Burns. It now appears to be used as a holiday cottage. Here they lunched and sketched, and observed an interesting social phenomenon, on which Victoria commented:

'We crossed the burn at the bottom, where a picturesque group of 'shearers' were seated, chiefly women, the older ones smoking. They were returning from the south to the north, whence they came.'

Seasonal work, in fishing, shearing and other areas, was a vital source of employment in the impoverished Highlands at this time. These women had probably returned from taking in the harvest – it was October – in Lowland Scotland, in the Lothians and elsewhere, and were returning home, on foot. Poverty as much as lack of transport meant that they walked south to the hairst, and later walked back.

After lunch the party moved on a little to the White Well, and drank some of the water which Victoria described as 'very pure'. In an absurd piece of iconography, a commemorative structure was later built here to mark the blessings the water received at the Queen's lips, and it was renamed the Queen's Well. The well marked another drovers' stance, before the route southwards. The well still springs, and it is sweet and cold.

Lord Dalhousie had met the royal party on Mount Keen, and now took them past the manse to his new shooting lodge. Victoria admired the scene in which,

'...the old *Castle of Invermark* came out extremely well; and, surrounded by woods and corn fields in which the people were 'shearing', looked most picturesque... the old ruined castle [is] half covered with ivy.'

At the lodge itself she surveyed Loch Lee, with its 'wild hills at the back' – before again getting 'into our carriages... a sort of double dog-cart which could carry eight', and driving down the glen. The weather was closing in, as 'the mist and rain seemed to come down heavily over the mountains', but in the glen it was bright as they drove. Viki noted a new Free Church at Tarfside, showing she was aware of the theological issues in the Kirk surrounding the Disruption of 1843. She was more partial than her Ministers liked to Scotch religion (as she was to Scotch whisky), and her attendances at Presbyterian worship in Crathie were thought by many to be unseemly for an Anglican head of state. There was just time before it got dark to have a wee stroll along the riverbank at the Burn, and admire the woods and the 'curious narrow gorge... with deep pools, completely overhung by wood'.

Though arriving in Fettercairn in the dark, the day's excitement was not yet over. They stayed at the Ramsey Arms, clean and tidy to the Royal liking, and no complaints this time about the food – 'a very nice, clean, good dinner', with Brown and Grant changing the plates nervously at table. After eating, they went out in the moonlit night for a stroll, with no sound but the barking of a dog. But –

'Suddenly we heard a drum and fifes! We were greatly

alarmed, fearing we had been recognised... Still, as we walked slowly back, we heard the noise from time to time, and when we reached the inn door we stopped, and saw six men march up with fifes and a drum (not a creature taking any notice of them), go down the street and back again.'

On asking in the hotel what it meant, they were told it was 'just a band' which walked about that way twice a week. I am certain Victoria found it better amusement than what they had been doing previously – reading charity proclamations stuck on the Mercat Cross! The loyal burghers of Fettercairn, despite the fact that Vikki had sneaked through *incognito*, raised a commemorative arch to her visit in 1864; it doubles the things to look at in the town.

The return journey the following day took the group over the Cairn o Mount (*Cairnie Month*) back to Deeside, passing en route properties including that of the Gladstone family at Fasque. William Ewart Gladstone was already beginning to dominate British politics and was to be Prime Minister in 1867. Victoria did not like him, 'He talks to me like I am a public meeting,' she famously commented, preferring his Conservative opponent Disraeli, who, like John Brown, knew how to ingratiate himself with the Queen, describing his tactics as 'trowelling on the flattery'.

Driving on a good road, they crossed the Feugh, passed Finzean (pronounced Fingan), and Marywell, which Vikki apparently didn't know was named for its associations with Mary Queen of Scots, before arriving on the south side of the Dee at Aboyne. But instead of simply driving home along the Dee, they decided to link up with their route of the day before, by heading up Glen Tanar. Again, new carriages are waiting as if by magic!

'We crossed the Tanar Water, and drove to the left up Glen Tanar – a really beautiful and richly-wooded glen, between high hills – part of Lord Huntly's forest', wrote Vikki. They drove about six miles to their lunch spot 'which was very pretty', probably about where the present Half Way House stands, and then after a short walk they drove on again, in threatening weather, to

*Eatnoch* [Etnach], 'a keeper's house in the glen – a very lonely place, where our ponies were'. However pleasant it was to have one's life organised by a cast of hundreds, an unpleasant incident took place at Etnach, and Victoria, though undoubtedly possessing humanity, could become quite uncharitable when something spoiled her rural idyll. She comments:

'A wretched idiot girl was there by herself... a good deal bent, and dressed like a child, with a pinafore and short cut hair. She sat on the ground with her hands round her knees, rocking herself to and fro, and laughing...'

General Grey prevented the royal presence being contaminated by the girl, interposing himself between the idiot and the Queen, and an old man then arrived to take her away. From Etnach, Victoria returned to the Bridge of Muick by the way she had come, over Polach Hill.

A rather more unpleasant incident had taken place at the Etnach some time previously. When the Baron o Brackley went out to fight Inverey, according to the ballad he had only his brother as an aide, while Inverey had 33 men. The result was a foregone conclusion.

At the heid o the Etnach the battle began
At little Aucholzie they slew the first man
First they slew ae man and syne they slew twa
The baron o Brackley is deid and awa.

(Aucholzie pr.= Auchoozie.)

The lands of Glentanar, however, remained in Gordon hands after Brackley's demise, centuries later being bought by a rich English eccentric, William Cunliffe-Brooks, who littered the place with innacurate plaques and clusters of estate buildings in the English rural vernacular. Subsequent to this, though hardly an improvement, Glen Tanar passed to the Coates family of Paisley, whose fortunes were made in thread manufacture (Coats Paton). As well as pretentiously changing the name of the estate to *Glentana*, the Coateses tried to restrict access through the old Mounth road by erecting gates at the entrance to the glen and harassing walkers in the 1920s. A court case, supported by the Rights of Way Society and Aberdeen County Council, ended this attempt at coercion. The Coateses have now gone from *Glentana*, as their thread mills have gone from Paisley, and access problems appear to be a thing of the past.

## WALK 14: GLEN MUICK TO GLENTANAR (Map H)
### 12 miles, 4½ – 6½ hours

*Only the most dedicated monarchists would wish to slavishly follow in Victoria's footsteps, rather than using her travels as the basis for a good walk. I would suggest using the disparate parts of this expedition as the basis for two walks: one from Ballater to the Shiel of Glentanar and back, and one following the old Mounth Road. The former is a pleasant short day out, and takes the bulldozed track south from Ballintober near the Brig o Muick, over the hills, pasing south of Craig Vallich, before descending to the Shiel of Glentanar, now a ruin and a pleasant lunch stop, with a rough wee howff out the back for shelter. If you subsequently cross the Mounth, you will have more or less followed in Victoria's steps, though not in their order of making. (OS 44)*

There are problems in repeating the main Mounth walk in the footsteps of Queen Victoria – not forgetting the hundreds of drovers and shearers who went before, and for a while after her. If one carried out the walk in its entirety, one would either have the option of repeating it the same day, a retracing of footsteps which would involve a tramp of over 25 miles, with some steep ascent as well, or, for example, of starting from Glen Mark, overnighting in Aboyne, and returning southwards the next day. (Accommodation is difficult on the Glen Mark side of the Mounth Road.) A further option would be to be dropped at one end and picked up at the other, but this would involve the efforts of a partner prepared to drive a considerable distance. Envy Vikki, who did not have to think of such logistics!

## WALK 15: MOUNT KEEN (Map H)
### 15 miles, 6 – 8 hours

*Whatever is decided, this walk is a splendid one, and for the most part takes place on bulldozed tracks which make route-finding easy and walking swift if sair on the feet. On the gradients these tracks have turned into horrendous water courses, with savage erosion taking place – it is absurd that there are no planning restrictions over such estate-sponsored vandalism to the environment. Starting at the car-park in Glen Muick, six miles of land-rover track takes you to Corie Bruach. Only crossing Mount Keen itself does the track become a footpath, still generally good and clear. Here one should take the high road and bag the peak, not the low road possibly taken by Victoria. Though not in itself a peak of great merit, its isolated position gives Mount Keen wonderful views of Lochnagar and the Cairngorms in clear weather – and even the multi-storey flats of Aberdeen. The descent into Glen Esk, and further towards the road end, is without problem. (OS 44)*

# The Last Big Trip

Few would deny that autumn is the finest season in the Highlands, and especially on Deeside, with its frosts, clear days, trees turning and the heather in bloom. Victoria's prose was generally, well, prosaic, but occasionally she could describe what she saw in a quietly attractive way. Thus, of 6 October 1861 she wrote:

'To our great satisfaction it was a most beautiful morning. Not a cloud was on the bright blue sky, and it was perfectly calm. There had been a sharp frost, which lay upon parts of the grass, and the mountains were beautifully lit up, very blue shades upon them, like the bloom on a plum.'

Vikki liked this latter phrase, and repeated in it her account.

Once more the party headed for the mountains, reaching Loch Callater from Balmoral via Braemar, by a road described as 'very bad indeed as we approached the loch' in about two hours; it would appear that the general rate of travel was less than ten miles an hour, a fine speed for sightseeing, and Albert apparently liked Glen Callater very much. At the loch Victoria mounted her trusty pony Fyvie, and they set off. Never very accurate in her route descriptions, on this expedition there are special problems with Victoria's geography. She says they set out, ascending *Little Cairn Turc* and then *Cairn Turc* itself [Carn an Tuirc] 'on the north side of Loch Callater', when the mountain lies demonstrably to the south. She found the ascent, 'up a sort of footpath, very easy and even...' and from the flat summit admired Lochnagar and Ben MacDhui, 'the shape of which is not fine'. The ascent of Carn an Tuirc had clearly taken the north-east shoulder of the mountain whence they 'looked down upon *Loch Canter* [Kander] ...very wild and dark'.

From thence, they proceeded southwards, to a hill called by Victoria *Cairn Glashie*. This can only be Cairn of Claise, and here the party dismounted and Victoria, like all good Victorians, gives a minute description of 'the wonderful panorama stretched out before us', which I will spare the reader, though it does indicate that she kent her bens, identifying such divergent peaks as Schiehallion and Ben Nevis. Another half hour's riding brought them to, in Vikki's words, 'a bonny place', which she gives as *Cairn Lochan*. Because she tells us that the River Isla flows through it, can we deconstruct this as Caenlochan; later there is a reference to *Ca-Ness* which indicates the spot where luncheon was taken as being Druim Mor which hangs above the cliffs of Caness Glen. This would correspond with the description given as follows: 'We sat on a very precipitous place, which made one dread any one's moving backwards.' They had a very acceptable lunch there, as the air was very keen; Brown took some of the ice 'thicker than a shilling' they found on the summit of Carn an Tuirc in his hand and it did not melt. Albert obviously felt he should perform a trick or two as well, so while Vikki sketched, he left a message in a Selters-bottle, and buried it in the ground. (I wonder what the message said – maybe 'Bugger that Brown, will no one rid me of the man?')

The return trip took place in falling light, which Victoria delighted in observing and describing. The 'mountains became clearer and clearer, of a lovely blue, while the valleys were in shadow.' She liked using local dialect words in her descriptions, and here says she cannot 'mind' all the hills they climbed that day, though we can work them out. They returned to Cairn of Claise, then headed south west over the head of Garbh Choire and ascended *Glass Meall* [Glas Maol]. From there they took the *Month Eige Road* [Monega Road] to the Spittal Bridge on the Cairnwell road. The descent from Glas Maol took place down the old Monega Pass, the highest of the Mounth Roads. Here Victoria had problems – 'it was so wet and slippery that I had two falls' – though generally she doesn't dwell on such mishaps. She had more problems with Sron na Gaoithe (nose of the winds), which becomes *Aron Ghey* in her account. But having traversed Cairn an Tuirc, Cairn of Claise and Glas Maol, Victoria's final tally of Munros (she did no more) would appear to be eight.

Victoria observed that a new road was being built over the Cairnwell in 1861. Coaches traded the route from Braemar to Perth at this time, and Victoria had crossed the Cairnwell road herself on 15 August 1849, describing the journey from the Spittal of Glenshee as follows:

'The next stage of 15 miles to *Castletown* is over a very bad, and at night positively dangerous road, through wild, grand scenery, with very abrupt turns and steep ascents. One sharp turn is called The Devil's Elbow.'

They had enjoyed the expedition in 'quite a different direction from any that we had ever made before', and Vikki was pleased that it 'delighted dear Albert'. Already aware of her Consort's failing health, she finished the *Journal* with the words, 'Alas! I fear our *last* great one' – adding in an 1867 postscript 'IT WAS OUR LAST ONE!' When they left Balmoral, Broon remarked that he hoped there would be no deaths in the royal family. Albert died in December, and this convinced Victoria that Brown was psychic, and even that he could communicate with Albert beyond the grave; the consortual succession was being prepared. Despite being in some quarters a feminist icon, Vikki was really the fish that needed the bicycle. Melbourne, Albert, Broon...

If you are doing your Munros, but can't quite get excited about all those heathery rounded tops east of the Cairnwell Pass, why not re-invent it as an historical walk in Victoria's footsteps? These stories Vikki would, I'm sure, have been delighted to hear, had anyone had the wit and knowledge to inform her.

On the way up Glen Callater, Craig Phadruig is passed on the left, and behind it lies the eponymous loch. Here in former times a priest from Braemar prayed for the severe frost to end to restore the people's water supply; his prayers were, as in all good stories, answered. The Braes o Mar remained one of the isolated pockets of Highland Catholicism long after the Reformation, and indeed from the evidence of the Statistical Accounts, it was only in the early 19th century that Protestantism became the dominant religion. Even today there is still a strong Catholic community in Braemar, whose church played a part in a mountaineering tragedy.

In January 1959, a party of hillwalkers from a Glasgow Catholic walking group left Braemar hostel to walk over the Tolmount pass to Glen Doll, an unwise decision at that time of year, especially with bad weather forecast. An even unwiser decision was to turn back after they had started, and return to Braemar to attend Mass; this was fatal, as it meant the ensuing delay found them at the wild summit plateau as the worst of the storm hit, the party having passed Glen Callater itself. Three days later their five bodies were found on Jock's Road, on the Glen Doll side of the pass. So do not underestimate these rounded hills; in blizzard conditions their very featurelessness makes route-finding harder, as many have found, though, like the Jock's Road casualties, not living to tell the tale. As a line from an old poem has it, 'I daur ye gang yer lane till dark Glen Doll!'

Before descending, you cannot fail to notice the dreadful eroded mess at the summit of the Cairnwell pass, caused by attempts to develop downhill skiing in a country whose climate does not favour such initiatives. Victoria saw this area as we can no longer, as it was when the pass was a fearsome obstacle to north-south travel. Try and block out the image of car parks, cafés and ski tows, and imagine the area below Meall Odhar as it was in 1644.

## WALK 16: THE MONEGA MUNROS (Map I)
### 15-20 miles (acc. to route chosen), 6 – 10 hours

*The road from Auchallater farm to Loch Callater is now much better than in Victoria's time, a land rover track going to the former small shooting lodge above the loch, where there is also an open bothy providing shelter. Indeed the road is too good, for the Invercauld estate has bulldozed an unsightly track to a considerable height over the old path which rises up the northern shoulder of Carn an Tuirc and which Victoria took. Hopefully National Park status for the Cairngorms will include outlying areas like Glen Callater, and restrictions will be imposed upon the landowners' sacred rights to damage the environment. You leave the bulldozed track behind and gain the summit of Carn an Tuirc. The rest of her route is easy to follow, though from Cairn of Claise you might wish to take a diversion to the Tolmount to bag another Munro, as much as to see and try to imagine where the walkers in 1959 began to fatally run out of luck. Return to Cairn of Claise by Tom Buidhe, and a further peak has fallen. Another short diversion from the summit of Glas Maol will get you the summit of Creag Leacach; six Munros in one day, and fairly easy ones at that. You will doubtless wish to descend by the historical Monega Road, to the military bridge built over the Cluanie water in 1750. It is still four miles from the foot of the Monega pass to Auchallater where this walk began. There are no sociables waiting for today's walker to ease the pain on the feet of this section, the sting in the tail of a day with an easy half-dozen Munros ascended. (OS 43)*

A party of Campbell raiders were returning from plundering Glen Isla and Glen Shee, when they were ambushed on the slopes of the mountain by those bent on retaliation. One of these was an archer from Braemar, called Cam-Ruadh (the one-eyed, red-haired man). His deadly arrows turned the battle against the Campbells, who fled leaving their *spulzie* (plunder) behind. Arriving home to his loyal wife, who had his supper ready for him, Cam-Ruadh was greeted by the cry, '*Chaim Ruadh, Chaim Ruadh, tha saighead na do thoine!*' (Cam Ruadh, Cam Ruadh, you have an arrow in your arse!). As he unconcernedly continued eating, she pulled it out for him. There is no record of Vikki performing a similar set of tasks for her man after one of his hunting expeditions, though she would doubtless have enjoyed the story of Cam-Ruadh.

## *The Social Construction of Virtual Reality*

The feudal escape on Deeside was about landscape and architecture, but also about social relations. The bigger picture of a neomedieval life did not simply involve castles, hills and heather, but was constructed from a totality of experiences, from the recreational to the religious. Let us look briefly at Kirk, Kulture and... the Kames at Praemar.

I'm not suggesting Albert wanted to restore every feudal bond, including the *jus primae noctis* on his Deeside estate – in fact Vikki kept him so busy in that department that I doubt the lethargic Albert would have been up to it; maybe that is the reason he was always 'tired'? But he and Vikki both felt that worshipping with the peasants at the local Church was important – as had the nobility in feudal times – and this public worship was not normal royal practice, indeed was frowned upon by many in the household and senior staff. Additionally, as nominal head of the Church of England, and therefore an Episcopalian, Victoria broke with tradition by attending Presbyterian worship in the Kirk of Scotland.

It is clear, too, that the practices of Presbyterianism appealed to Victoria, and her entries on the Kirk in her *Journal* are most complimentary. On 29 October 1854 she wrote, 'Went to Kirk, as usual, at twelve o'clock. The service was performed by the Rev Norman Macleod, of Glasgow... and anything finer I never heard. The sermon, entirely extempore, was quite admirable; so simple, and yet so eloquent, and so beautifully argued and put.' The simplicity of Presbyterian worship appealed to her, and she clearly found extempore sermons more uplifting than the prescribed ritual of Anglicanism. The next year she attended a service given by 'The Rev J Caird, one of the most celebrated preachers in Scotland...' who 'electrified all present by a most admirable and beautiful sermon, which lasted nearly an hour, but which kept one's attention riveted.' Anglican divines must have shuddered with horror in reading of 'electrifying' sermons, which were quite outwith their tradition, smacking as they did of religious 'enthusiasm' of the kind which had given rise to civil war in England in the 17th century.

In 1843 the Disruption had occurred in Scotland. About half of the Kirk's ministers and members left, in protest against the right of landowners and town councils to 'present' a minister for approval or not by the congregation. The Free Kirk defended the traditional right of congregations to 'call' ministers themselves, without the influence of 'patronage'. The Free Kirk was quite strong in rural Aberdeenshire, though never dominant in the way it was in the West Highlands, and there was a congregation at Ballater. Victoria was aware of the issues surrounding the schism, but as patron herself of the Crathie and Braemar parish, her sympathies probably lay with the 'Auld Kirk', as it became known; certainly she never worshipped in a Free Kirk.

The Auld Queen kept going to the Auld Kirk till the end. Indeed, when the need for a new building became apparent, Victoria gave a considerable sum to the total of £6,000 needed for its building, as well as hosting a bazaar in Balmoral to raise funds. A bizarre bazaar it was too, with various fledgling royals running stalls selling discarded regal bric-a-brac alongside peasant donations of lace and venison, and agricultural equipment. On 18 June 1895, Victoria was present at the official opening of the new Kirk, which is the one standing today and with which her descendants still have strong connections. It was designed by Alexander Mackenzie of Aberdeen, and despite the use of local materials, is rather more elaborate in its exterior and interior details than the average Presbyterian Kirk. It is apparently open to visitors.

Various other social rituals bonded the classes together in the feudal pyramid in the never-never-land of *Brigadee*. There was watching the peasantry at work. On 13 September 1850, Victoria and some others went to watch their tenantry catching salmon. At this time salmon was not a game fish, jealously protected; in fact, it figured on the menu of Aberdeenshire farm hands so much that they would threaten to quit work unless better fare was provided. The rod and line were still some way off, and salmon were effectively but unsophisticatedly caught by *leistering*. The river was netted, and men with leisters, a kind of trident, drove the fish towards the net where they were killed. Vikki comments: 'It all had a very pretty effect; about one hundred men wading through the river, some with kilts, all very much excited.' Even Albert got in and had a go, though 'he caught nothing'. A man almost drowned in the leistering, but was rescued. Then there was 'juicing the sheep', which Vikki observed at the Bush, the farm of John Brown's brother near Crathie. On 21 October 1868 she drove over to watch the process, done to preserve the wool. The sheep were dipped in liquid tobacco and soap which was boiled over a fire in a cauldron by 'a very rosy-faced lassie... It was a very curious and picturesque sight,' she concluded, without feeling the wish to roll up her sleeves and get to work herself.

More exalted activities were, however, not lacking. The Duff family, proprietors of the Mar estate, gave a torchlight ball on 10 September 1852 at the old Mar Lodge at Corriemulzie, the present lodge not being built till 1895. This event epitomises the whole ethos of Balmorality; let us leave Vikki to describe it.

'It was really a beautiful and most unusual sight... A space about one hundred feet in length and sixty feet in width was boarded, and entirely surrounded by Highlanders bearing torches, which were placed in sockets, and constantly replenished. There were seven pipers playing together, Mackay leading... There were about sixty people, exclusive of the Highlanders, of whom there were also sixty; all the Highland gentlemen were in kilts...'

There were sword dances, and reels, including one by eight Highlanders holding torches in their hands. It was all pronounced worth seeing and admirably done, with Albert delighted. (A *Journal* footnote states that the Duffs were now 'Earl and Countess of Fife'; well, they worked for it. In 1899 Princess Louise, daughter of the Prince of Wales, married the sixth Earl of Fife, who owned a quarter of a million acres with a rental of almost £80,000 per annum. Vikki approved of the match, 'as he is immensely rich'.) But return to the quotation and look at that phrase: sixty people, exclusive of the Highlanders... it speaks volumes.

Vikki appears to have liked torchlight events, for she expressed a desire to see the locals keeping Hallowe'en. In 1866 in an ecumenical union, Catholics and Protestants celebrated the event on the same day, so Vikki could see it to maximum effect. 'We went upstairs to look at it from the windows, from whence it had a very pretty effect.' The next year she took a more active part. After being out driving, the party met the participants with their torches on return, and Vikki joined in a procession round the house, led by Ross the piper, and followed by the mass of locals carrying torches. 'After this a bonfire was made of all the torches, close to the house, and they danced reels whilst Ross played the pipes.' I cannot imagine that the local Presbyterian minister approved overmuch of this royal enthusiasm for the relics of superstition, as he would have viewed the Hallowe'en celebrations.

But the main feudal ritual, binding the classes in an organic union, was of course The Games, today a place of pilgrimage for monarchist devotees. That Highlanders indulged in games is not in dispute. That games took place a thousand years ago at what is presently Braemar, with Malcolm Canmore present, is not in dispute either. But to attempt to draw an organic bond of continuity between these facts and the present Gathering is to do violence to the historical process, for in almost every respect these Games are a 19th century invention. In terms of their tartans and their dress codes, the current Highland garb was created in the last century, as indeed were many – though not all – of the games themselves. Even the Highland bagpipe of today was developed for the regiments of the British Army, and is a different instrument from that played in the pre-1745 Highlands.

After the '45, all clan gatherings for social and sporting occasions were banned, as being covers for rebellion; pipes, tartan and weapons, as well as the Gaelic language, were also banned. Most of these measures were unenforceable, and were repealed in 1782, by which time the Highlanders' enthusiasm for fighting for the Hanoverians in their colonial wars had begun to turn the clansmen in the popular mind from rebels to heroes. In 1800 three Braemar 'vrichts' (wrights, probably carpenters or blacksmiths) marched through the town and engaged in some friendly sports. In 1817, taking advantage of a lessening of restrictions on workingmens' associations, they formed the Braemar Wrights' Society, an organisation which collected dues for the relief of sickness, unemployment and widows of members. In 1826 it became the Braemar Highland Society and instituted a Wrights' Walk, in which members, led by a piper, marched to a spot and engaged in athletic activities.

Soon the local lairds were in on the act, subsidising the games, and offering space for their performance. This was not entirely disinterested, or unique. All over Scotland at this time there was a revival of sport, which many saw as a means of social control, and a method of ensuring that the minds of the lower orders were occupied with non-radical thoughts. The fabulously rich Earl of Eglinton, a Tory whose wealth ironically came largely from mining in Ayrshire, re-invented many medieval games and by means of pageants tried to spread them amongst the Ayrshire working classes in the 1840s. One of his tournaments was attended by 100,000 people from all over Britain – unfortunately, almost all middle and upper class. Later factory owners, quite unwilling to provide decent working conditions, were enthusiastically funding works' sporting organisations and bands: as well as keeping minds off socialist radicalism, these advertised the philanthropy of the capitalist and his product in a way hygenic toilets did not. Interestingly, many radical working class politicians of the 19th century saw drink and sport as the two evils which kept the working man in a state of mental servitude.

The Braemar Games might have died out, six hundred miles from civilisation in Disraeli's words, but for the accident of *Brigadee* (as indeed did the games re-invented by MacDonell of Glengarry at roughly the same time which included a tug o war aimed at dismembering a live bull). Victoria first attended the games when they were held at Invercauld in September 1848, beginning an association which culminated in royal patronage being extended to the games in 1866. In 1850 she attended the games held that year at Braemar Castle, and left us the following description:

'There were the usual games of 'putting the stone' 'throwing the hammer' and 'caber', and racing up the hill of Craig Cheunnich, which was accomplished in less than six minutes and a half; and we were all much pleased to see our gillie, Duncan, who is an acive, good-looking young man, win... It is a fearful exertion... eighteen or nineteen started, and it looked very pretty to see them run off in their different coloured kilts...'

Poor Duncan, however, spat blood after the event, and according to Victoria, 'he has never been so strong since'. This event, which certainly dates back to Canmore, was discontinued. After the games there was dancing in the castle.

The games continued to circulate until 1906, when the present site in Braemar was acquired. But they also spread, first downstream to Ballater in 1864 and then to Aboyne in 1867, thence all over Scotland, and even into the industrial Lowlands. Doubtless in some cases the cause was the emigration of Gaels to the towns, but the games were held in places where few Gaels settled, and must be seen as part of the general Celtification of the image of Scotland at this time, an image which was encouraged by the upper classes, with their mental icons of grouse moors and loyal hielan' laddies dying in far flung corners of the Empire. (Interestingly, it did not work the other way. Burns Clubs remained an entirely Lowland phenomenon, with not one established north of the Highland line.) Indeed, with their subsequent spread worldwide, Highland games probably do more than any other single factor in determining foreigners' image of Scotland as a country. It is an amazing phenomenon, without parallel culturally. Imagine if the defeated South, which had played the minor part in the evolution of the USA till then, had become the dominant cultural reference in the post-Civil War USA; if foreigners had the impression of the USA as a vast Dixie, with happy negroes 'singin on dem plantations', and noble landowners looking after their interests. Such a switch happened in the image of Scotland from about 1830 to 1880, and Victoria gave it the royal stamp of approval. Whether it would have happened so speedily and so totally without her influence, is another question.

The last social ritual to be observed by the *grand signeur* is of course delivering alms to the poor, who are always with us. In September 1857 Vikki 'stopped at the shop and made some purchases for poor people and others', then visited a few old women, giving them warm petticoats or a dress and a handkerchief. Clearly Vikki was the gainer in all this, as the old women poured out effusively their gratitude and love for their monarch. 'It was very touching', Vikki notes, and worth a few coppers no doubt. (As Margaret Thatcher said, it is good to be rich, because you can be charitable – a virtue denied to the poor.) Such charitable activities, to an ever grateful populace, continued right till Vikki's death.

For Victoria, for the aristocracy, and increasingly for the bourgeoisie, the creation of a mythical Highlands was a solace from the uncertainties, ugliness and threats of industrial society, and especially its still uncertain element: the working class. Away in the Highlands there was manly endeavour and feudal loyalty, the imagined 'real' world set against the perceived 'artificial' world of elsewhere. But this Highlands of theirs was a fabrication, a virtual reality where the residual population dressed up and played games for their masters, and the actuality for the rest was poverty and emigration.

# CHAPTER 5

# The Long Goodbye:
# Mrs Brown's Travels

THE FOUR DECADES BETWEEN Albert's death and Victoria's own were spent by her in an extended farewell to the spirit of her Consort, a long goodbye where he is mentioned at every possible juncture, and mourned effusively as well. But mourning didn't become Victoria, and one has to suspect that much of her grief was simply attitudinising. It is hard to credit that a woman of spirit, with all her faults, could grieve sincerely for forty years for the apology for a man that was Albert. At the risk of sounding ungallant, or politically incorrect depending on the historical perspective, it is difficult not to believe that the Mother of her People was having the Mother of all Menopauses. But she had her consolations. Earlier she had tended to confuse Albert and God, now she could confuse John Brown with Albert as the image of flawless male perfection. The film *Mrs Brown* implies that Broon was not very prominent pre-1861, and mainly a servant of Albert's. In fact, as Victoria wrote in 1861,

'...for the last three years he has been my personal servant here and always attends me when I go out – walking, riding and on all our travelling expeditions. He is an excellent, handy servant, able to do anything.'

In 1865 he was elevated to the rank of 'The Queen's Highland Servant', and in a footnote to the *Leaves from the Journal of Our Life in the Highlands*, dated 1867, she wrote in praise of the man who was already arousing resentment and rumour,

'His attention, care and faithfulness cannot be exceeded... He has all the independence and elevated feelings peculiar to the Highland race, and is singularly straightforward, simple-minded, kind hearted and disinterested; always ready to oblige; and of a discretion rarely to be met with' – *Broon*? I wonder if Vikki would have thought any different of her 'loyal Highlander' had she known that his ancestors possibly came from Fife.

Victoria continued to travel extensively in Scotland, indeed with the spread of the railway system she travelled even more than before, visiting areas like the West Highlands previously difficult of access. These journeys were, however, more in the nature of tourist trips, as she seldom ventured far from the road or rail carriage. Even at Balmoral, her trips became less adventurous, consisting of pilgrimages to places previously seen with Albert, and generally from the comfort of wheeled vehicles. Though it still has interest, these limiting factors make *More Leaves from the Journal of a Life in the Highlands* (1884) a less absorbing work than its predecessor. The first edition of 10,000 copies quickly sold out and was reprinted; but one should compare this with the purchase of 240,000 copies in a month of Gladstone's *The Bulgarian Horrors and the Question of the East* in 1876 as an indication of the priorities of the Victorian reading public.

## Balmoral without Albert: Mourning becomes Victoria?

Although Albert had now departed the estate where he had terrorised generations of deer, he was not to be forgotten, Victoria was on that determined. Almost as if she feared forgetting him, she began to litter the place with mementoes to her former husband. On 26 August 1862, Albert's birthday, she went 'to see the obelisk building up to His dear memory' (Albert was now designated with the capital H of deity). As if this was not enough, five years later on 16 October 1867, 'Our blessed engagement day!', a statue to Albert was unveiled at Balmoral, though the covering caught as it was pulled off, and the falling rain dampened spirits. But for Vikki it was worth it, for 'we gazed on the dear noble figure of my beloved one, who used to be with us here in the prime of beauty, goodness and strength.' John MacAdam, the Scots radical working man, called these monuments 'vain memorials for doing nothing' – which is possibly charitably expressed. Later Victoria was to add a statue for Brown, another for Battenberg, one for Prince Leopold, commemorations of faithful dogs... the place became a virtual mausoleum.

One can only feel that Vikki protested too much when she stated that she could no longer bear to visit Allt na Guibhsaich, her *bothie* where she and Albert had often stayed, insisting instead, in a magnificent piece of attitudinising, that a new dwelling be built for her, the Widow's House at the far end of Loch Muick, the Glas-Allt Shiel. (Interestingly, she didn't claim that *Balmoral itself* was too full of sad memories...) On 1 October 1868 it was officially opened. On a frosty evening they drove by Birkhall, and arrived at half past six at the new building which met with royal approval, 'so cheerful and comfortable, all lit up and the rooms so cozy and nice'.

After dinner, there was a party, with all the servants, which Vikki did her best to spoil. 'Five animated reels were danced in which all (but myself) joined.' Whisky-toddy was brought round, to drink to the 'fire-kindling' of the house, and to Victoria's health. Brown had to beg that she would take some, but she does not record if she acceded to this particular request of his. After an hour she went off to bed, but hinted that the men went on singing for some time in the stewards' room afterwards. Meanwhile Vikki recorded her 'sad thoughts', and that she was missing 'her darling husband' – not for the first or the last time. Even the Glas-Allt Shiel is an Anti-Memorial to Albert. Victoria liked Scott; she should have pondered on his novel *The Antiquary*, where a poor fisherman whose child has died is back at work next day. When chastened by a pair of his rich social superiors, he replies that if he was not so employed, his other children would die of hunger, and that only the rich can afford public displays of grief. Vikki didn't have the fisherman's problem, and could wallow – and recriminate. Though Albert had died of typhoid, she blamed her son Bertie's bad behaviour with women and gambling for having killed his father.

The first recorded trip in *More Leaves* is interesting, because in it an accident occurred which revealed how ill-prepared royal personages were for initiative. Vikki was persuaded to drive 'with a heavy heart' to *Altnaguithasach* where they lunched on soup and tatties, riding afterwards to the summit of the Capel Mounth in light snow showers. They were rewarded with a fine view, but even in recording this, Vikki felt obliged to remind us of her mourning:

'All the high hills white with snow; and the view over the green Clova hills covered with snow at the tops, with gleams of sunshine between the showers, was very fine, but it took us a long time, and I was very tired towards the end, and felt very sad and lonely.'

After taking tea at Allt na Guibhsaich, the carriage started back, but in the dark the driver appeared to lose the way, and in the confusion the carriage toppled over and the royal party were 'coupit oot', suffering very minor injuries. Such an incident however, to people who lived choreographed lives, becomes a major disaster, and Victoria melodramatically 'had time to reflect whether we should be killed or not' as the vehicle overturned. While the driver was sent off for a replacement carriage, the party simply sat in the overturned vehicle and waited. There seemed to be no idea that they might expedite their rescue by, for example, walking down the road. Vikki commented, in the Marie-Antoinettish manner she often employed, 'A little claret was all we could get either to drink or wash my face and hand.' Was there nae watter in the burn that day? After half an hour of this torment, the ponies arrived and they rode down to the distillery, where a new carriage was waiting. During all of this ordeal, Vikki was sustained by thoughts of Albert: that she was following his precept of making the best of everything, that the accident had not occurred due to any deviation from what he might have sanctioned and approved, and so forth. And she was reassured when Princess Alice told her cloyingly that 'I am sure he [Albert] watched over us.' Lord Palmerston, the Prime Minister, warned Victoria against future rides which might end in darkness; she refused to give up the practices of her darling Albert... however Smith, the driver in this case, was sacked and pensioned off soon afterwards. Broon became the hero of this incident, the saviour of his monarch, as he was often later seen by Vikki, whether protecting her from Fenian assassins or troublesome paparazzi. She liked her men manly.

Though generally becoming less adventurous, Victoria did indulge in overnight trips from Balmoral after Albert's demise. But without her husband, or maybe it was just having reached a certain age, Victoria lacked the light-heartedness of former days. A trip to Tomintoul on 24 September 1867 illustrates this. Victoria drove with her companions by Glengairn to *Cock Brigg* as she calls it, using local nomenclature. 'Then came a very steep hill, the beginning of very wild and very grand scenery', she comments, which was the start of the crossing of the Lecht Road, built by General Wade. On the descent of a 'very wild pass', she observed that the road is very bad, and that, 'Near... are iron mines belonging to the Duke of Richmond'. These were actually mainly lead mines, and the ruins of the buildings can still be seen, forming a pleasant short walk from the Lecht Road of less than a mile on a good track. Victoria does not comment on seeing the memorial to the building of the road at the Well of Lecht, but does again observe a drove of 'very fine Highland cattle', which indicates the continuing use of the road for such a purpose, and a possible reason for its bad state.

They carried on past Tomintoul, on which Vikki appears to have mellowed since her last visit, saying it 'lies very prettily among the trees', and continued in a more or less whisky country tour, mentioning 'the celebrated Glenlivet distillery', and passing such centres as Knockandhu and Tomnavoulin. An attempt to have a picnic near Ben Rinnes was abandoned because of rain, and then after driving through Dufftown, another distilling centre, the party entered Glenfiddich. Vikki did not visit the distillery, or any of the other instruments of material production which she passed on her travels – mines, quarries and so forth – as they lacked the romantic glamour she was seeking. The scenery of Glenfiddich pleased her, but on arriving at the lodge, there is consternation when the Duke of Richmond (later of Gordon) is not there.

But there is a much greater kerfluffle when it is discovered that though the servants have arrived, the luggage, last seen toiling up Glen Gairn, where it had stuck till helped on by four farm or cart horses, was still missing.

'We waited and waited till dinner-time, but nothing came. So we ladies.... had to go into dinner in our riding skirts... I, having no cap, had to put on a black lace veil... None of the maids or servants had any change of clothing.'

What is all the fuss about? They can hardly have worked up much of a sweat sitting in their carriages. Is this the Vikki of yesteryear, who mucked in and was 'always content'? Later there is more fuss as bedtime approaches. News comes that the luggage is at Tomintoul, and a rescue party is sent out, followed after midnight by Brown, 'who was indefatigable' and who goes out on a further luckless luggage search. Victoria tells us that she 'disliked the idea of going to bed without any of the necessary toilet. However, some arrangements were made which were very uncomfortable.' One hesitates to speculate what these were! She finally fell asleep through fatigue at three in the morning.

This incident shows again how the smallest interruption in the ritual of royal life causes untold and disproportionate anxiety. So much luggage was taken for this trip that four borrowed horses, in addition to those originally attached, could hardly pull the carriage containing it up Glen Gairn. As well as armies of Victoria's and Richmond's own servants, and the myriads of coachmen, a rough count reveals that this fairly minor trip involved four changes of horses, as well as the bringing along of the royal ponies, which were not used. For one minor royal outing! But such extravagance was repeated all over the Highlands at this time by the aristocracy and the bourgeoisie on their estates, while in the industrial lowlands millions of people were without the basic human needs of adequate food and shelter, and had more to worry about than whether the three changes of clothing needed in a day were at hand.

Shorter trips became the order of the day, and one took place on 3 October 1870, the day Vikki gave her consent to the marriage

## WALK 17: GLENFIDDICH (Map F)
### 14 miles, 5 – 7½ hours

*The walk up the estate road to Glenfiddich Lodge is an easy and pleasant outing, and can be extended by taking Morton's Way, a 19th century hunting road built by a tenant of that name, to Corryhabbie Hill, which was the main base for the early trigono-metrical surveys of Scotland. The Way starts a little past the lodge, and takes a right turn southwards. (OS 28 and 37)*

of Princess Louise to Lord Lorne, one of the Campbell progeny. She heard of the proposal on returning from a trip to Pannanich Wells, the mineral spa which lies a couple of miles from Ballater on the south side of the river, and to which the town owed some of its original prosperity. Despite the fine weather, she found an air of desolation about the place as 'almost all the trees which covered the hills have been cut down'. Vikki notes too that the wells 'used to be very much frequented', indicating that by then their glory days were past. However, 'We got out and tasted the water, which is strongly impregnated with iron, and looked at the bath and the humble but very clean accommodation in the curious little old inn...'. Even here, Brown gets a look in, and she mentions that he 'stayed there for a year as a servant'. The fame of the wells began in 1760 when an old woman was cured of scrofula by their waters, and they were developed by one of the Farquharson gentry, keen to utilise the economic potential of his estate. After many years, the waters of Pannanich are now once again available commercially.

The last entry in the second volume of Victoria's *Journal* shows us Vikki in a tender, female bonding role. The Empress Eugenie was having a hard time. The wife of womaniser Napoleon III, she had followed him into exile in Britain when he was overthrown by the republican revolution which followed the Franco-Prussian War in 1871. Napoleon subsequently died, but his son, rather superfluously given the title the Prince Imperial, joined the British Army, and fought in the colonial wars in Africa. He was killed by a party of Zulus, and the news reached Victoria on 19 June 1879, the tidings brought by Brown. Vikki wrote the next day, 'Had a bad, restless night, haunted by this awful event, seeing those horrid Zulus constantly before me, and thinking of the poor Empress...'. A bit unreasonable, perhaps, to call the Zulus 'horrid' since, although the Prince was there in a non-combatant role, the Zulus, unused to such military etiquette, were not to know that he was not trying to kill them. So Vikki invited Eugenie to Balmoral, and took her a wee drive for consolation.

On 6 October they went to the Gelder Shiel, or the Queen's Shiel, which lies north of Lochnagar and has a magnificent view into the north-east corrie of the mountain. 'The evening was perfectly beautiful, warm, and clear, and bright', Victoria mentions, and they walked a mile and a half or so above the Shiel with the dogs, chatting 'about former times'. Brown had meanwhile been busy and 'had caught some excellent trout and cooked them with oatmeal, which the dear Empress liked extremely...'. They had fine weather for their picnic 'It was a glorious evening – the hills pink, and the sky so clear.' The Empress 'was pleased with the little Shiel', and after tea, drove to Abergeldie where she was staying.

Actually Vikki herself was an Empress by now, and a real one, not a deposed one. As part of his continuing plan to raise the profile of the monarchy for the benefit of the Conservative party and social order, Disraeli had made Victoria Empress of India in 1876 (after all, her daughter would one day be Empress of Germany, and Vikki couldn't be left behind in the Title Race!). Victoria loved the elevation, and was a jingoistic defender of British imperial interest, writing to Dizzy (now Lord Beaconsfield) in July 1879, 'If we are to maintain our position as a first rate power... we must with our Indian Empire and large Colonies *be prepared for attacks and wars, somewhere or other*, CONTINUALLY.' To every adventure of British Imperialism for a half century, from the Crimean War to the Boer War, she gave enthusiastic and public support; she just loved handing out medals.

The Shiel is no longer occupied by royalty, but the ruinous byre close by was used for many years as an open bothy by

## WALK 18: GELDER SHIEL (Map E)
### 9 miles, 3½ – 5 hours

*The walk to Gelder Shiel from Balmoral is a pleasant one of less than ten miles round trip, on a good land-rover track, giving fine views into the corrie of Lochnagar. Starrting from Easter Balmoral, you pass through the valley of the shadow of death, obelisks to the right of you obelisks to the left of you, before a left turn takes you southwards over open moorland; as the path approaches the Gelder Burn, another left turn takes you to the Shiel, which has long been visible. You can vary the return by taking the path alongside the Gelder (ruined clachans) back to a weir, where a right turn brings you back to the obelisks. (OS 44)*

climbers, before being restored by the Mountain Bothies Association, and it continues to provide primitive shelter. Here in 1966 an encounter occurred between a gang of republican anarchist desperadoes and Queen Elizabeth herself, accompanied by her royal entourage at a picnic – which constituted my first royal audience. We were staying in the bothy which was bedecked with a huge charcoal slogan 'BAN MONARCHY', when Lizzie, some of her bairns, and some servants arrived. We were leaving anyway, as we explained to the mediating menials and the very nervous armed guard. The second royal audience was less accidental. In 1968 Mike (my pal) and I were aiming to sit in front of Harold Wilson's car at Crathie Kirk, with a banner saying 'STOP SUPPORTING US AGGRESSION IN VIETNAM'. But we missed him, and ended up on our doups in front of the Queen Mither's car, with her giving us wee daft waves, and the monarchist wifies hitting us with their handbags. The bobby gave Mykee a wee doing, then let us go. But we got on the front page of the *New York Times*.

The trip to Gelder with Eugenie ends the second *Journal* and the explorations of Deeside, but the trips to other areas of Scotland are also of historical and social interest, and to these we now turn.

**View in Glencoe (1801) by J. Merigot**
(Aberdeen Art Gallery and Museums)

Merigot's is one of the earliest paintings from this vantage point, looking towards Bidean nam Bian; later Turner and McCulloch would follow in his brush-strokes. Before the deer forest, cattle – as seen here – were the monarchs of the glen. Victoria's picnic, spoiled by the journalists, took place roughly at this vantage-point below the Three Sisters, and she stated, 'we had a splendid view of these peculiarly fine, wild-looking peaks, which I sketched.'

**Beinn a' Ghloe (1819) by George Fennel Robson**
(Aberdeen Art Gallery and Museums)

Robson noted a cairn on the summit of Beinn a' Ghloe, and this was possibly erected by the party of General Roy, who first ascended and measured the height of the mountain in 1776. With the development of the deer forest later in the nineteenth century, the Duke of Atholl attempted to close, unsuccessfully, a right of way over the shoulder of the mountain. Victoria first viewed Beinn a' Ghloe from her ascent of Carn a' Chlamain in 1844.

**Ben MacDhui (1819) by George Fennel Robson**
(Aberdeen Art Gallery and Museums)

Remote MacDhui was not climbed until the visit of Rev Dr Keith in 1810, when he carried out the barometric measurements which dethroned it from its pre-eminence amongst British mountains, a verdict disputed by many on Deeside for long afterwards. Victoria climbed MacDhui in 1859, remarking on the "truly sublime and impressive" situation of the mountain. This view is up Glen Luibeg.

**Ben Nevis (1819) by George Fennel Robson**
(Aberdeen Art Gallery and Museums)

Various attempts had been made to climb Nevis before James Robertson ascended the mountain in 1771, to investigate its economic potential. Thereafter it became, after Ben Lomond, the most popular Scottish mountain for tourists to climb, accessible as it was by boat. Victoria first passed by the Ben in 1847, and returned in 1873, when she had the fortune to see Nevis 'all pink and glowing in that lovely after-glow (Alpengluhen), which you see in the Alps. It was glorious.'

**At the Head of Glen Torridon (c1870) by George Washington Wilson**
(Aberdeen Art Gallery and Museums)

Wilson's first love was painting, and he clearly had talent, as shown in this study of Liatach, which was done not long before Victoria visited Wester Ross in 1877. This was a remote area, with few of its mountains climbed. Victoria was astounded by 'the dark mural precipices' of 'savage-looking' Liatach, commenting that because of their steepness, 'The mountains here... seem so much higher than our Aberdeenshire mountains'.

**Highland Gathering at Balmoral (c1850) by Sam Bough**
(Aberdeen Art Gallery and Museums)

The Braemar Games date from 1817, when artisans organised competitions for charity, but by the mid century the event had been taken over by the Deeside landowners, who hosted it in rotation. Here it is the turn of the Queen to mount the pageant. Balmorality in pure form. A romantic neo-feudal never-never land of Lords and peasants, arrayed in an invented Celtic costume, and engaging in 'Highland' games, many of little historical validity. The revival or invention of sports in the Victorian period was seen as a buttress to the social order, mingling ranks and absorbing minds that might otherwise go astray.

## Pottering in Perthshire

Victoria did not push the boat, or rather the barouche, out much in the years after Albert's death, but in 1865-6 she made a couple of visits to her *neebers* in Atholl. On 9 October 1865 her party took post-horses to Braemar and then over the Cairnwell Pass to the Spittal of Glenshee. It was a miserable day and the way seemed long, as it would at the speed of a horse-drawn carriage.

After leaving the Spittal they turned into Strathardle, arriving at Pitcarmich, where the Duchess of Atholl was waiting for Vikki, and where they lunched. Thereafter their troubles began, caused partly by poor weather and bad visibility. They were aiming to take their ponies across an old drove road which goes from Strathardle through wooded, hilly countryside to Dunkeld, where a 'cottage' had been prepared for the Queen. In pouring rain they passed *Little Loch Oishne and Loch Oishne* [Oisinneach Bheag and Oisinneach Mhor], before coming to Loch Ordie, where they sheltered, dried out and had some tea and whisky at the lodge. Although the worst part of the journey was past, and they were accompanied by Atholl men who knew the way, it was now dark, and they got lost. 'I must own, I was somewhat nervous,' states Victoria, '...and I was much alarmed, though I would say nothing.' One cannot help thinking that the Vikki of old might actually have enjoyed the adventure of being lost in the hills...

As the road deteriorated, it was clear that the coachman was confused, and the Duchess had no idea where they were either, having taken a timber road instead of the usual path. Pushing on, they eventually saw a light, and found they could proceed to Dunkeld, where they arrived at the 'snug little cottage' just before nine o'clock. The cottage, of course, was a virtual palace.

Victoria was not very energetic on this trip. The day after arrival she went to the dairy to look at some cows, after having afternoon tea with the Duchess. It was a wet day, and so was the next one (the weather seemed to deteriorate after Albert died). Vikki spent a morning fashing over Broon, who had cut his leg on his wet kilt, but in the afternoon the weather cleared and they

## WALK 19: KIRKMICHAEL TO DUNKELD (Map B)
### 15 miles, 5½ – 8 hours

*This is a pleasant walk, though daytime and good weather will make yours a preferable experience to that of Victoria. At Kirkmichael in Strathardle, beside a ruined kirk, the road heads southwards over moorland, passing the two Lochans Oissineach amongst pleasant woodland. Then it descends the Brackney Burn to Loch Ordie, and south to the curiously named Santa Crux well. Thence one can take the road back to the main road at the Loch of Butterstone, but a more pleasant route which takes you directly to Dunkeld is to veer westwards on the track which goes through the woods to Mill Dam, a while afterwards reaching a car park near the road. Monarchists should do it at night, in the rain. (OS 52 and 53)*

took a drive to the Lochs of the Lowes, commenting, 'They are surrounded by trees and woods, of which there is no end, and are very pretty.' Then, in order to make the best of the day, they drove further, and passed through Dunkeld and Inver to the Hermitage.

'This is a little house full of looking-glasses, with painted walls, looking on another fall of the Braan, where we took tea almost in the dark. It was built by James, the second Duke of Athole in the last century.'

The Hermitage, sometimes called grandiosely Ossian's Hall, was built in 1757, and a romantic Ossian's cave was constructed upstream, the whole being surrounded by an exotic tree garden, an early example of the Celtified Romantic nonsense becoming fashionable amongst the idle rich. A few years after Victoria visited it, the Hermitage was badly damaged by an explosives attack, and the authorities were never able to discover the culprits, faced by a wall of silence in Dunkeld and surrounding district.

One should not take the apparent loyalty of the Highland inhabitants to their social superiors at its face value. The Dukes of Atholl were in constant conflict with local people, over access rights for example, but the Propaganda by Deed undertaken against the Hermitage was more likely concerned with the Dunkeld Bridge controversy which occurred around this time. Telford had built a bridge across the Tay at Dunkeld in 1809, replacing the ferry-crossing which the Highlanders had sought to capture in 1689, and a beautiful and useful construction of seven arches the briggie is, too. However, like the Skye Bridge, it was a Private Finance Initiative, most of the money being put up by the Atholl family, and heavy tolls were levvied on every item of menial or bestial which passed, iron toll-gates being constructed for the purpose of collection.

Once the railway line opened in 1856, passions rose, as every time a traveller from Dunkeld passed over the bridge to the station and back, tolls were exacted. People from Birnam, on the railway side, paid tolls to go to church in Dunkeld. In the general atmosphere of social unrest surrounding the passing of the Second Reform Act in 1867, passions boiled over, and in 1868 a large crowd, armed with axes, attacked and demolished the toll-gates, throwing them into the river. Order was only restored when a detachment of the 42nd Royal Highlanders was brought in to quell the riots. The tolls were abolished in 1879. Maybe there is a lesson in these events for the opponents of the iniquitous tolls on the Skye Bridge... But, back to Vikki.

On their final full day, the Queen visited Dunkeld Cathedral with the Duchess. A centre of remote Christianity from Celtic times, she describes it as follows: 'part of [it] is converted into a parish church, and the other part is a most picturesque ruin. We saw the tomb of the Wolf of Badenoch, son of King Robert the Second. There are also other monuments, but in a very delapidated state.' She says no more about the cathedral, and goes for a wee stroll on the banks of the Tay – but Dunkeld had its part to play in the ultimate replacement of the Stuarts by the Hanoverians.

In 1689 the clansmen of Claverhouse had won a great victory over the troops of King William at Killiekrankie in their attempt to restore James II to the throne. But Clavers was killed, and buried at Old Blair. The Highlanders then advanced towards the Lowlands, and at Dunkeld met the newly-formed Cameronian

Regiment, fanatical Calvinists and haters of the Stuarts, under their commander Colonel Cleland. Though Cleland was killed, the Cameronians stopped the Highlanders' advance by fortifying the cathedral and town of Dunkeld, and forcing the Highlanders into street-fighting, a kind of warfare they were not good at. In the battle the cathedral was damaged and its roof stripped for bullets; many houses were set on fire also, deliberately to confuse the Highlanders. It is a little-known battle, but as important in its way as Sheriffmuir and Culloden in that it ended the first of the three Jacobite Rebellions. (Cleland lies buried in the Cathedral.)

In the afternoon Vikki went for a wee hurl on a coble (a type of boat) on Loch Ordie where the adventure of their late arrival at Dunkeld had taken place. A rather less adventurous route was taken homewards to Balmoral the next day (Friday the 13th), by Ballinluig, Edradour and along Strathardle to Kindrogan. On this route Vikki, ever-mountain responsive, commented on the 'beautiful view of the hills, Schiehallion, Ben Lomond, Ben Lawers' – though I personally am doubtful if she could have seen Ben Lomond from Strathardle. There was an adventurous sting in the tail to this journey, as they took the hill road from Kindrogan by Diranean to the Spittal, which rises to over 2,000ft. Possibly this road was in better condition in 1865 than today, but even so Victoria had to dismount at the summit, the *Larich* [An Lairig], and walk down to the Spittal, worrying all the time about Brown's inflamed leg. The ascent appears to have been reasonably straightforward, though, and after reaching the summit, a brew-up *al fresco* was organised, where Vikki insisted that all the party take a hot toddy. At the Spittal, carriages were waiting as ever.

On her return trip to the 'cottage' the following October, Victoria repeated an awful lot of the ground covered in 1865. She drove back over the Spittal-Kindrogan road (where she interestingly remarked that in Strathardle Gaelic was still widely spoken in 1865), had tea again with the Duchess (when she saw a capercailzie), visited the Lochs of the Lowes *again*, and came home by the route of misadventure in 1865 via Loch Ordie – and to avoid the ennui of repetition we will not follow her, or take the reader,

## WALK 20: SPITTAL OF GLENSHEE
### 12 miles, 4½ – 6½ hours

*This is a straightforward walk, short enough to be reversed in a day and thus avoiding logistical problems. Starting at Enochdu the road to Diranean is taken, and then followed (signposted) through Calmanach wood on a good land-rover track to the open moor. Passing Elrig (an old deer driving spot), it climbs steeply to An Lairig, and deteriorates somewhat; from the summit it is a brief and swift descent to the Spittal (tea stop), before returning by the same route. This is an old road, shown on General Roy's Military Survey of the 1750s. (OS 43)*

over the same terrain. She did, however, cover new ground on 3 October 1866, and made a drive of over seventy miles into the heart of the Perthshire countryside, which is worth the recounting.

Taking the word of the Duchess that the weather would improve, Vikki set off and crossed the Tay bridge in mist and drizzle. They then proceeded along the west bank of the Tay to Dalguise. A little beyond Balnaguard, where Vikki had changed horses in 1842, she complained peevishly that, 'Now an unsightly and noisy railway runs along this beautiful glen, from Dunkeld as far as Aberfeldy.' It is all in the eye of the beholder: at Dalguise there is a beautiful latticed iron railway viaduct, resting on piers flanked by fine masonry towers, enhancing the landscape in the opinion of most. They continued past Grandtully Castle, at that time rented as a shooting lodge by an India Maharajah, Dhulep Singh, and entered Aberfeldy, 'a pretty village opposite Castle Menzies... among fine, high-wooded hills', but did not stop to go for a walk in the famous Birks o Aberfeldy, celebrated in Burns's poem.

Vikki had a quick look at Taymouth, where she had been so regally received in 1842, when 'Albert and I were only twenty-three, young and happy', before proceeding through Kenmore where there was a fair in progress and along Loch Tay to Fearnan. She reminisced about her row on the loch with Gaelic-singing boatmen on her previous visit; now Kenmore and Killin were linked by steamer. The route of 1842 was taken again, through Fortingall, but then at Keltneyburn a new country was entered, taking the old Wade road, constructed in 1730.

'We then passed the village of Coshieville, and turned by the hill-road – up a very steep hill, with a burn flowing at the bottom, much wooded... passed the ruins of the old castle of the Stewarts of Garth, and then came on a dreary wild moor – passing below Schiehallion, one of the high hills...'

Of interest hereabouts, but not visited by Victoria, is the huge Tomphubil lime kiln, built in 1865 at the summit of the road, tapping a rich source of the material for agricultural improvement, and still in good condition. Also at the Schiehallion (Brae of Foss) car park is a memorial to the Astronomer-Royal, Nevil Maskelyne, who conducted experiments on the mountain in the 1770s to determine the density of the earth, possibly climbing to the summit with General Roy, the military map-maker.

The party descended to Tummel Bridge, and then drove back along Loch Tummel, stopping at a place already called The Queen's View 'though I had not been there in 1844' comments Vikki acidly. Locals, encouraging tourism, invented Prince Charlie's Caves all over the place; was there a similar illicit trade in Queen's Views? But the place was cursed; stopping to have a picnic, Broon couldn't get the kettle to boil, 'and the tea was not good. Then all had to be packed, and it made us very late.'

This meant that when they passed Killiekrankie, 'It was fast growing dark... from the lateness of the hour and the dullness of the evening – for it was raining – we could hardly see anything.' Passing through Pitlochry, they changed horses, but other irritants interceded; plaids fell off, the coachman's light went out, and all in all they got home very late. But, despite the mishaps, Vikki pronounced it 'a beautiful and successful journey', and 'a very interesting day'. Pottering amidst the pleasures of Perthshire appears to have roused her interest in travelling in Scotland, and other trips soon followed.

# The Wattie Tour

Walter Scott had been responsible for bringing the first Hanoverian monarch to Scotland, by organising the visit of Victoria's forebear, George IV, in 1822. Scott was not directly responsible for bringing Vikki north, but bears some indirect responsibility, for the Queen was an avid reader of his poems and novels, and she based much of her favourable preconceptions of the country on her reading of Scott. It is therefore surprising that she took so long to pay homage to the Wizard of the North, since his home at Abbotsford was well-established on the tourist circuit. This was rectified in 1867.

This was Victoria's first big Scottish tour largely by train. The line had reached Ballater in 1866, adding to the prosperity of the town, and Victoria now started coming to Deeside twice a year by train. Tourists, and increasingly climbers like those of the later-founded Cairngorm Club, used it for access to Deeside. The line operated for exactly one hundred years, and featured delightful stations, with wooden fretwork much in evidence. The one at Ballater survives as a tearoom and Railway Museum, and is well worth a visit.

Vikki travelled south to Carlisle by train, and then her carriage was attached to another train and taken on the now disused line by Liddesdale to Kelso passing *en route* 'the Eildon Hills, three high points rising from the background', one of Scott's favourite spots. Victoria found the scenery fine. 'The country is extremely picturesque, valleys with fine streams and trees, intermingled with great cultivation.' But it does not seem to have inspired her in the way that the Highland scenery did.

At Kelso station she was met by various big wigs, including the Duke and Duchess of Roxburghe, the Chookie Buccloo, and General Hamilton ('commanding the forces in Scotland'). And in the town there was an outburst of orchestrated monarchical fervour:

'...there were triumphal arches, and no end of pretty mottos, and every house was decorated with flowers and flags. Fifty ladies dressed in white strewed flowers as we passed. Volunteers were out and bands were playing... a little girl was held up to give me an enormous bouquet.'

After this she passed to Floors Castle, where she indulged in a little Albert weepiness: '...the feeling of loneliness, when I saw no room for my darling, and felt indeed I was alone and a widow, overcame me very sadly.' Lunch and planting a tree helped cheer her up.

The next day, Victoria was escorted to the ruins of Melrose Abbey, where they 'got out and walked about the ruins, which are indeed very fine, and some of the architecture and carving in beautiful preservation.' Here, though references to specific points like the Eildons show that he was in her mind, she makes her first reference to Scott, quoting his lines:

> If thou wouldst view fair Melrose aright
> Go visit it by pale moonlight

– and, 'Another twenty minutes or half-hour brought us to Abbotsford, the well-known residence of Sir Walter Scott.'

Vikki's first impressions were not favourable. 'It lies low and looks rather gloomy' she wrote. But she enjoyed the house tour. And an incident showed her admiration for the author.

'They showed us the part of the house where Sir Walter lived, and all his rooms – his drawing room with the same furniture and carpet, the library where we saw his ms. of *Ivanhoe*, and several other of his novels and poems in a beautiful handwriting with hardly any erasures, and other relics which Sir Walter had himself collected. Then his study, a small dark room, with a little turret in which is a bust in bronze, done from a cast after death of Sir Walter. In the study we saw his journal, in which Mr Hope Scott asked me to write my name (which I felt it to be a presumption in me to so do), as also the others.'

Finally they visited the dining room where Scott had died, and Vikki records that 'we took tea'. On the journey home they passed 'the old tower of Smailholm', near which Scott had passed some of his childhood.

The next day it was rideabout time, and the Queen visited

Jedburgh 'very prettily situated', and 'full of historical recollections'. She had 'a good view of the old Abbey, as curious in its way as Melrose'. They drove further 'through a beautiful wooded valley up the Jed, in the banks of which, in red stone, are caves in which the Covenanters were hid.' This is possibly a surprising piece of information for Victoria to have, as the Covenanting image of Scotland was fading fast before the more romantic Jacobite one. But she was versed in Scots ecclesiastical history past and present, noting as she was leaving Floors for the night train from Kelso that 'The Free Kirk, a pretty building was lit up with red light, which almost gave it the appearance of being on fire.' Before nine next morning she had returned to 'our dear Balmoral'. Homage had been paid, but the Borders could not compete with Balmoral for Victoria.

## The Trossachs (or Rob Roy) Tour

Vikki had enjoyed her Wattie trip, but in a restrained way; the Scott she really liked was not the Border one, but the Highland one, and before long she had a chance to renew aquaintance with an area which Scott had often written about. On 1 September 1869 she left Balmoral for the train at Ballater, 'Brown as always, unless I mention to the contrary, on the box'. Was this Mrs Brown, sneaking away with him whom the press was already calling 'the Queen's stallion' for intimate communication? Hardly, for with them was Vikki's Secretary, first Colonel, later General, Ponsonby, as well as 'Emilie Dittweiler and Anne MacDonald, Ocklee (for the girls), Jane Churchill's maid, Charlie Thomson, and the footman Canon, went with us. Blake, Spong with the luggage, A.Thomson with Sharp (my faithful collie dog) and Anne Gordon (house-maid), Kennedy, Arthur Grant, and Hiley (the groom) with the ponies all went yesterday, and three cooks came from London'. Despite this huge cast, when they were having luncheon on the carriage 'we could have no one to help to pack and unpack it...'. Could they not have done it themselves?

The train took them to Callander, where 'We at once got into our celebrated sociable. Which... had been sent on before...' They drove through the village which the Queen remarked had 'very few shops' and many poor houses, and drove along Loch Venachar, noticing 'Ben Venue and other high and beautiful mountains' before coming to Invertrossachs, which Vikki describes as 'small and comfortable' – at this time it had about two dozen rooms! She noted with approval that 'they have put down new carpets everywhere'. The owner of Invertrossachs, Lady Macnaghten, had graciously vacated the house for Vikki, and had been told not to 'go to any unnecessary expense' but of course, had.

The next day Brown drove the party in the sociable back towards Callander where Vikki noted 'Ben Ledi, a splendid hill...', and then they headed south by the road past Loch Ruskie and the Lake of Mentieth, of which Victoria commented, 'The country about here is rather lowland...'. However, once at the Clachan of Aberfoyle, 'renowned in Sir Walter Scott's *Rob Roy*', things improve, 'and here the splendid scenery begins – high, rugged and green hills... and Ben Lomond towering up before us with its noble range.' They were favoured with good weather, Vikki saying it was 'very hot', and remarking at one point they could see the Wallace Monument at Stirling. While sketching, she noticed 'some poor little cottages with picturesque barefooted lasses...', adding, surprisingly, for we are only twenty miles from the Second City of the Empire, that 'All speak Gaelic here.'

They drove along Loch Ard 'which reminded me very much of the drive along Lake Zug in Switzerland' to Loch Arklet, 'on the banks of which Helen Macgregor is said to have been born'. Indeed Vikki adds that 'The scene of our drive today is all described in *Rob Roy*.' Arrived at Stronachlachar, they waited for the steamer, which, ironically a mere century after the hanging of one of the outlaw's sons had finally pacified this area, was called *Rob Roy*. In the glorious evening sunlight, Vikki became quite ecstatic and got carried away, stating:

'This solitude, the romance and wild loveliness of everything here, the absence of hotels and beggars, the independent simple people, who all speak Gaelic here, all make beloved Scotland the proudest, finest country in the world. Then there is the beautiful heather, which you do not see elsewhere. I prefer it greatly to Switzerland, magnificent and glorious as the scenery of that country is.'

Flattering though this may be to Scottish self-perception, it hardly represents the reality of industrial, urban Scotland in 1869, or even of the Highlands themselves.

In fact Victoria is so uplifted, that when she boards the *Rob Roy*, she mentions almost in passing that she and her 'beloved Husband' had previously sailed on it when they opened the Glasgow Water Works in 1859 – though at the landing place 'which I remembered so well; ...very melancholy and yet sweet were my feelings'. She recalled that Albert had collected some pebbles there to make a bracelet for her. She collected a few more. On the sail itself she notes 'the rugged Ben Venue', adding, again showing that Wattie was more with her on this trip than Albert, that the mountain was 'so famed in the 'Lady of the Lake' (which we had with us...)'. Indeed, Vikki again is inspired to quote from Scott's poetry,

Each purple peak, each flinty spire
Was bathed in floods of living fire.

After a splendid evening's drive in the gloaming, the Queen, though 'very tired', pronounced this 'A most successful day'.

Next day saw the party again on the *Rob Roy*, this time heading up the loch to Stronachlachar, and then driving along Loch Arklet towards Inversnaid on Loch Lomond. The development of Scotland's tourist industry was indicated by Victoria's comment that (it was a Saturday) 'We met (as we had done from the first) several large coaches... full of tourists.' Arriving at the inn at Inversnaid, Victoria was taken by the scenery, which again reminded her of Switzerland. At Inversnaid there was only one house, the inn, but previously there had been a Redcoat barracks for suppressing Jacobitism and banditry. The area had been visited by the poet Gerard Manley Hopkins, who composed a poem entitled 'Inversnaid', but it is doubtful if his poetry would have been to

Vikki's taste, which inclined more towards the iambic pentameter. Albert had visited Loch Lomond in 1847, and the steamer Victoria's party boarded was called... the *Prince Consort*. 'A pleasant idea that that dear name should have carried his poor little wife', comments Victoria rather cloyingly.

Victoria was impressed, as indeed it is difficult not to be, by the sail on the Loch. 'We steamed southward, and for the first half nothing could be finer or more truly Alpine, reminding me much of the Lake of Lucerne...' They passed Ben Lomond 'well wooded part of the way, with cornfields below'. The woods are still there, but cultivation on that side of the bonny banks is a thing of the past. She showed a detailed interest in what she observed, such as that on Inchcloanaig island the Bruce encouraged the planting of yews for use in archery, though again she is a little disappointed by the southern end of the loch where 'the shores become much flatter and tamer'.

However they proceeded northwards after lunch, and Vikki came in sight of what she had already the previous day designated as 'the splendid Alps of Arrochar', where were found the 'highest and finest mountains, with splendid passes, richly wooded...'. In particular she observed 'that most singularly shaped hill called the Cobbler'. They steamed further to the head of the loch where 'the mountains here are peculiarly fine from the sharp serrated outline and wonderful clothing of grass and trees' and where she attempted to sketch, being 'much vexed' that the boat was going so fast. Scott's bandit makes an appearance again when Vikki is shown a hole in the rock 'which they called Rob Roy's cave'. But just when the reader is thinking that it is safe to come out of the water, we have the obligatory, 'How dearest Albert would have enjoyed it!' Vikki, he would probably have been sea-sick.

Victoria stayed another couple of days at Invertrossachs, but the only notable event was an incident at the Brig o Turk, where she visited Fergusson's Inn, which she said 'is in fact the very poorest sort of Highland cottage' – continuing,

'Here lives Mrs Fergusson, an immensely fat woman [Vikki was no sylph herself. I.R.M.] and a well-known character, who is quite rich and well dressed, but will not leave the place where she has lived all her life selling whisky. She was brought out and seemed delighted to see me, shaking hands with me and patting me. She walks with a crutch, and had to sit down.'

What an opportunity for a blether! What tales Mrs Fergusson would have had to tell! But someone like Vikki, with her rigid upbringing, was unable to do more with such people than exchange meaningless pleasantries, or receive homage, and sadly she writes, 'We only stopped a very few minutes...'. So instead of Mrs Fergusson's memories, we have from this trip a detailed account of who occupied which rooms at Invertrossachs... It is interesting that on these occasions, Broon's room appeared never to be very far from that of Vikki – make of that what you will.

Loch Katrine still forms the main water supply for Glasgow, and while virtually every steamer has gone from virtually every other loch in the Highlands, the *S.S. Walter Scott* still plies the waters of Loch Katrine in the summer months, and is indeed available to hire for celebratory occasions. You can therefore take Victoria's sail to Stronachlachar and fancy yourself Lady, or Lord, of the lake. Many people take bikes on the boat and then cycle round the head of the loch and back along the north shoreline, where there is a very good road, metalled most of the way; but it is possible to walk it, of course. Alas, there are no longer charabancs from Stronachlachar to Inversnaid.

## The Clearances (or Powsowdie) Tour

What Victoria saw is often interesting; what she did not see is frequently more so. This becomes very clear on a trip she made in 1872 to Sutherland, which of all areas in the Highlands had suffered worst from the effects of the clearance of people for sheepfarming. Thousands were expelled from the glens such as Strathnaver, and the ensuing suffering, and the death of an old woman when her house was set on fire, led to the trial of the factor of the Sutherland estates, Patrick Sellar. Marx later wrote,

'My lady Countess resolved upon... transforming the whole

tract of country into sheep-walks. From 1814 to 1820, these 15,000 inhabitants, about 3,000 families, were systematically expelled... All their villages were demolished and burned down, and their fields converted into pasturage... An old woman refusing to leave her hut, was burned in the flames of it.'

In other Highland counties the population was expelled from the glens to the coast, but overall stayed stable; Sutherland was the only county where the population actually fell in the first half of the 19th century. Meanwhile the Sutherland family built massive palaces for themselves, like Dunrobin Castle.

Vikki's trips with Albert had tended to be private affairs, often attempting to maintain secrecy, but this was no longer the case. When Prime Minister in the 1860s, Disraeli had feared for the future of the monarchy in the period of Victoria's excessive mourning. 'The monarchy is in danger, from gradual loss of prestige,' he wrote to Stanley, 'people find out that they can do without a Court.' In the aftermath of the revolution in France, Republican clubs sprang up all over Britain in the 1870s, and anti-monarchist sentiment was expressed in many publications, like *Punch* (in the famous empty throne 'Where is Britannia?' cartoon, for example), *Reynold's Newspaper* and the *Pall Mall Gazette*. In the Commons, MPs such as Charles Dilkes criticised the 'waste, corruption and inefficiency' of the monarchy, proposing its abolition. Victoria's relationship with Broon was an easy target, and in 1873 the republican Scot, Alexander Robertson, alleged that the Queen had had a child by Brown and become his morganatic wife (i.e. no future king could be Broon's). The sexual and gambling indiscretions of her eldest son, Bertie, didn't help the monarchist cause either. Victoria was encouraged to take a more public role, and the trips around Scotland began to be more organised monarchist pageants than clandestine trips to the wild Highlands.

On 6 September she took the train to Aberdeen, and received the keys of the city and an address from the Provost at the 'immensely crowded' station. She then took a railway line 'totally new to me', the one to Inverness, and always with an eye for the hills noted Benachie and the Buck o the Cabrach en route. At Keith the

Banff Volunteers were drawn up on the platform, while at Elgin there is another loyal address, the station decorated with arches and flowers. 'No British sovereign has ever been so far north', says Vikki, though diehard Jacobite sentimentalists might disagree with her. Indeed, showing her awareness of the history which had brought her ancestors to the throne, she mentions Macbeth's meeting with the witches at Forres, and then notes, 'We passed Culloden, and the moor where that bloody battle, the recollection of which I cannot bear, was fought.' I will deal in the next section with her complex and contradictory attitude to the Stuarts.

At Inverness, whose position she thought 'lovely', they stopped for a mere ten minutes, but the previous preparations had taken much longer! The Provost, ' a fine looking man in a kilt', again presented an address, Cluny MacPherson was there with the Volunteers, and a number of galleries had been erected where there were seats 'filled with ladies'. Passing the Beauly 'frith' (a common spelling then) she arrived in Dingwall, which the royal eye managed to construe as looking like 'a village in Switzerland'. There were more addresses, flowers and presentations; Vikki is introduced to Sir J Matheson, Lord Lieutenant of the County (of Ross and Cromarty) a man who had made his money in the Chinese drug trade and whom she was to meet again in 1877. Behind the Sutherland splendour lay the evictions, behind Matheson's, countless ruined lives in China, but it would be unrealistic to expect Vikki to have even been able to grasp this. As Marx once said, the rich understand that there are rich and poor; what they do not understand is that the rich are rich because the poor are poor.

Suddenly, at Bonar Bridge, out of the engine pops the Duke of Sutherland himself, whom Vikki says had been 'driving the engine all the way from Inverness', though doubtless what Victoria means was that he had accompanied the engine driver. At this station, there appears to have been difficulty with the orchestration of monarchist passion, for Victoria writes:

'There was a most excited station-master who would not leave the crowd of poor country-people in quiet, but told them to cheer and 'cheer again', another 'cheer', etc., without ceasing.'

At Golspie they detrain, and are met by a detachment of the Sutherland Volunteers, and drive through the streets decorated with flowers and inscriptions, such as (in Gaelic) 'A Hundred Thousand Welcomes'. Also chosen was the text,

Better lo'ed you canna' be
Will ye no come back again?

– rather ironically, since these are lines from a Jacobite song, expressing the wish that Charlie comes back to overthrow Hanover.

Even Vikki could not find Dunrobin 'small', a designation she often gave places most would think palaces. This pile she found had 'a very fine imposing appearance', being 'a mixture of an old Scotch castle and French château'. There follows one of Victoria's usual descriptions of where everybody slept and what their rooms were like, which was almost a necessary ritual for her when visiting, but is unusually tedious for the reader. There is one inadvertently amusing comment on this occasion, however, when she remarks that 'Brown lives just opposite in the room... [which] was formerly the prison'. Doubtless just the place where many by now would have liked to see the overbearing servant, of whom Disraeli noted that everything to do with Victoria needed the 'approval of the two JBS' – John Bull and John Brown. And note how close he was to Vikki's room as well...

The next day Vikki pottered about in the grounds and in the house, commenting without irony that '[The Duke] is wonderfully plain and simple in his tastes'. In the late aftenoon they went a drive in a wagonette through the Uppat Woods and past the Pictish Tower, to the monument erected by the previous Duchess to James Loch, a factor who came after Sellar. This memorial states, doubtless accurately, that Loch liked the view from here, but more dubiously that his 'life was spent in virtuous labour for the land he loved' – for Loch was the architect of the policy of 'improvement' on the Sutherland estates; though he did distance himself from some of the actions of Sellar, Loch nevertheless defended forced evictions. On return from this pilgrimage,

Victoria and her companions stop 'to take our tea and coffee', but a judgement is at hand for 'we were half devoured by midges'. Those were not midges, Vikki, but the spirits of the evicted crofters punishing you for honouring Mr Loch.

The rest of this trip is also spent on iconographic activities. The next day, Victoria goes to lay 'the first stone of the memorial to be raised by the clansmen' (there were none left...) 'and servants to the memory of my dear Duchess of Sutherland, who was adored in Sutherland'. While in the afternoon,

'We drove to the top of Benabhragie, or the Monument Hill, on which is the very colossal statue of the Duke's grandfather, the first Duke, who married the Countess of Sutherland from whom this enormous property came. She died in 1839, and I remember her quite well as a very agreeable, clever old lady.'

This agreeable, clever old lady and her monumentally commemorated husband were and are reviled in Sutherland to an unrivalled degree. The evidence of Gaelic poetry and oral tradition, and later evidence to the Napier Commission in the 1880s on crofters' rights are part of the general testimony to this. When the patriotic Sutherland laird was attempting to recruit his loyal peasants for the Crimean war in the 1850s, he was told to 'Go and get your sheep to fight for you!', and today there are widespread demands to remove the offending statue from Ben Bhraggie. I refuse to describe a route to the summit, till the monument is gone. But if you are desperate, you can work it out from the map.

On the drive Brown found a sprig of white heather, which brought them luck, for when they stopped this time for their picnic, the midges left them alone. The view from the monument gave them a sight of far-off Ben Rinnes. Victoria had two exciting experiences at dinner; in the first 'the Duke presented Mr Stanley, the discoverer of Livingstone', and she once again showed her willingness to experiment gastronomically – 'We had some sheep's head, which I tasted for the first time on Sunday, and think really good.' But the irony of this again would have been lost on Victoria; she was eating the head of the animal which had replaced the people of Sutherland.

# The Jacobite Tour

Victoria was a constitutional monarch, or rather was little more than a figurehead monarch, so limited was the power of the Crown by her day. Indeed Bismarck, the German Chancellor, regarded Britain as one of the 'republics' since, unlike Russia, Austria and Germany, its monarchy was largely ceremonial in its functions. Nevertheless, Victoria occasionally expressed high-sounding ideas about the monarchy, but the belief that she was in power by divine dispensation was difficult to square with Victoria's knowledge that the English Parliament had replaced the Stuarts with the line from which she was descended, in the Act of Settlement of 1701, which became applicable also in Scotland under the terms of the Union of 1707. Here I should state my own case, republican though I am, that the replacement of the absolutist-inclined Stuarts with the constitutional Hanoverians was a great progressive step in British politics, laying the basis for the evolution in time of democratic government. It is just that that time is now past, and what was progressive two hundred and fifty years ago is no longer so today.

We have noted above that Victoria was aware of the significance of the Battle of Culloden in 1746, and she often makes asides in the *Journals* about the Stuart line which had preceeded her own. Her Jacobite Tour of 1873 shows her visiting many of the former Jacobite heartlands, and musing interestingly on her relationship to the Stuarts and their heritage. This journey, and the others around this time made by the Queen, shows how the railway network had made travel around the Highlands enormously easier than hitherto.

She took the train to Aberdeen, and travelled southwards to Stanley Junction, where the Highland Line was joined. Memories of Blair and Albert gave way to even more gloomy impressions of Dalnaspidal and Drumochter, 'fine and wild, but terribly desolate and devoid of woods and habitations, and so veiled by mist and now beating rain as to be seen to very little advantage.' However at Kingussie there were 'flowers, heather and flags' and Cluny

MacPherson, who seems almost to have become Vikki's official stalker, playing soldiers again. They then encarriaged, and drove 'through the very poor long village of Newton More' towards Cluny Castle, passing 'miserable little cottages and farmhouses', to arrive where she had been back in 1847 and nearly bought some property, Loch Laggan. This time the weather, though showery, was more favourable, and she is eloquent on the beauties of the area, the 'very grand scenery, with the high finely pointed and serrated mountains... the drive goes under birch, mountain ash laden with bright berries, oak, alders in profusion, and is really quite beautiful.' A picnic allowed the digestion of tea, and passing Ardverikie, old memories were mulled over. Further on Victoria notes 'the celebrated Parallel Roads..., which are very interesting to all geologists as being supposed to mark the beaches of an inland lake, which was pent back by a great glacier in Glen Spean, and subsided to different levels...'. But they were not of enough interest to Victoria to stop and go have a look. You should though.

At Bridge of Roy there was 'a triumphal arch with heather and inscriptions, pipers playing etc, and Highlanders as well as other people drawn up, but we unfortunately drove past them too quickly.' The inscription on the arch stated that the loyal Highlanders welcomed their Queen, and Vikki states that 'it was put up by Mrs MacDonell of Keppoch' – the latter's name indicating that she was descended from notorious Jacobites, as indeed was Cluny MacPherson. The rain began to fall again, it became dark, and after crossing desolate moorland, they came to Inverlochy, where 'all were glad to go to bed'.

Vikki was a fair-weather mountaineer, and on the morrow she must have been so glad she had not chosen Lochaber as her Highland residence, for like in 1847 the weather was bad. 'Mist on all the hills, and continuous rain!', she moaned. Presumably this must have continued, for nothing is recorded in the *Journal* until Friday the 12th, when after painting in the morning of what was described as a 'most beautiful sunshiny day', Broon took Vikki and some others for a wee hurl into the Fort. She mentions seeing the Ben Nevis distillery, the Belford Hospital and the Fort itself, where 'Glencoe came to take the oath to King William III'. The town did not impress her: 'Fort William is small, and, excepting where the good shops are, very dirty, with a very poor population, but all very friendly and enthusiastic' – so that's all right, then!

In the afternoon they drove to Achnacarry, seat of Cameron of Lochiel, where they were received by the man himself 'wearing his kilt and plaid' – it seems hardly anyone wore troosers when Vikki was around. He owned his own 'very small but nice screw steamer' in which he took the royal party for a sail up Loch Arkaig.

'We went about halfway up the Loch (which is fourteen miles long) and had not time to go further, to the disappointment of Lochiel, who said it grew wilder and wilder higher up. To the left (as we went up) is the deer forest; to the right he has sheep...

Both sides are beautifully wooded along the lower part of the fine hills which rise on either side, and the trees are all oaks, which Cameron of Lochiel said were the 'weed of the country' and all natural.'

Indeed, Locheil regarded them as weeds: he cut them down and sold them! There is no steamer on the loch today, though an estate steamer, the *Rifle*, continued to service the shepherding communities of the loch until the 1950s.

After landing back at the pier, where a piper was playing, they drove through the Dark Mile between Loch Arkaig and Loch Lochy, 'dark from the number of very fine trees which overhang it...', and 'We here saw the cave in which Prince Charles Edward was hid for a week.' Vikki always called him the Prince, not the Pretender or the Chevalier, which ruffled the feathers of many.

Later Ponsonby commented to the Queen of the significance of the day's events, that there was Lochiel, whose great-grand-uncle's support had been crucial to the launch of the attempt to overthrow Victoria's own great-great-grandfather in the rebellion of 1745, showing the Queen some of the scenes associated with Prince Charlie's wanderings. Said Ponsonby, 'It was a scene one could not look on unmoved' – and Vikki was moved, breathtakingly adjusting the focus on her geneology to square the circle:

'Yes; and I feel a sort of reverence in going over these scenes in this most beautiful country, which I am proud to call my own, where there was such devoted loyalty to the family of my ancestors – for Stewart blood runs in my veins, and I am now their representative, and the people are as devoted and loyal to me as they were to that unhappy race.' So, once again, that's all right, then.

The following day, the weather holding, it was decided to visit Glencoe. The drive from Fort William to Glencoe on a fine day, then as now, is a wonderful experience, and Victoria was almost lost for words. 'All was so bright and green, with so much wood, and the loch so calm, that one was in perpetual admiration of the scenery as one went along.' However, Victoria was also exposed on this run to the full extent of West Highland poverty:

'The cottages along the roadside here and there hardly deserve the name, and are indeed mere hovels, – so low, so small, so dark with thatch, and overgrown with moss and heather, that if you did not see smoke issuing from them, and some very ragged dirty old people, and very scantily clothed, dishevelled children, you could not believe they were meant for human habitations... There were poor little fields, fuller of weeds than of corn, much laid by the wet...'. After crossing the ferry, the Queen entered Ballachulish, scene at that time of a large-scale slate quarry, where Victoria again notes that the people are poor, though the 'miners' and the village are 'very clean and tidy'. She was introduced to Lady Beresford, owner of the quarries. But 'meeting the people' was not in Vikki's style.

Glencoe attracted Victoria because it was famed for its awesome mountain scenery. She was impressed again.

'A sharp turn in the rough, very winding and in some parts precipitous road, brings you to the first, wildest and grandest part of the pass. Stern, rugged, precipitous mountains with beautiful peaks and rocks piled high one above the other, two and three thousand feet high, tower and rise up to the heavens on either side... It reminds me very much of the Devil's Bridge, St Gothard, and the Goschenen Pass, only that is higher, but not so wild.'

She was also fascinated in a negative way because of the infamous Massacre of Glencoe in 1692, when the MacDonalds had delayed signing an oath of loyalty to William of Orange, and then their chief had gone to the wrong place to finally do so; the massacre was the outcome of this sequence of actions. Already in her first *Journal*, when she had sailed in 1847 past the entrance to Loch Leven, she had remarked on 'Glencoe, so famous for its beautiful scenery and for the horrible massacre of the MacDonalds, in William III's time'. Now she reflects on the 'unfortunate massacred MacDonalds', and the 'bloody, fearful tale of woe' – but comforts herself with hoping 'that William III knew nothing of it'.

Their picnic below the Three Sisters, where Vikki was sketching, was rather spoiled by the appearance of some early paparazzi, one of whom was eyeing the party through a telescope, with a view to gaining information for an article for the Scottish press. Broon did his macho bit, and asked the reporter to leave; strong words were used, the Queen noted. Upon the reporter saying that he had as much right to be in Glencoe as the Queen had, the loyal gillie threatened violence, which was averted when the reporter's friends came and led him off. Brown was obviously pleased with himself, and on return commented that 'he thought that there would have been a fight...' Vikki reports his behaviour without criticism, and one suspects that she was quivering with delight at the behaviour of her gallant knight in – if not armour, at least tartan. In *Mrs Brown*, Broon drove off the paparazzi, throwing their equipment away and laying them all low; the actuality was less dramatic and heroic, more of a male rutting session than a knight vanquishing his foes.

However, this example of journalistic incivility was more than compensated for by a piece of feudal loyalty back at Ballachulish, where 'a very respectable, stout-looking old Highlander stepped up to the carriage with a small silver quaich'. Apparently Albert had drunk whisky out of it in 1847, and the *bodach* wanted Vikki to do the same. Though she liked her drappie, the Queen felt obliged to record that 'I felt I could hardly refuse, and therefore tasted some whisky out of it, which delighted the people who were standing around.' Crossing the ferry, they drove back to Inverlochy on a fine autumn evening.

The next day was spent on a drive in Glen Nevis, which

Victoria found 'almost finer than Glencoe'. They drove up the glen four miles to 'the base of Ben Nevis' and at the last habitation got out and walked a little further, but 'the road became so rough and bad' that they halted. It would appear that they stopped short of Nevis Gorge, of which no mention is made, and which could hardly have been missed by the party. Later Vikki admired her favourite collie, Noble, describing him as affectionate and biddable, never eating or moving without permission, and begging if he thinks he is out of favour.

Monday 15 September was devoted to the last leg of the Jacobite Tour, a trip to Glenfinnan where the standard had been raised in 1745 to launch the Rebellion.

After painting and a spot of lunch, they drove to Glenfinnan and Loch Shiel 'with very fine rugged hills on either side'. However, she is not impressed by the memorial, lately erected. 'At the head of the loch stands a very ugly monument to Prince Charles Edward, looking like a sort of lighthouse surmounted by his statue, and surrounded by a wall.' Now a dead cause, the romance and glamour of Jacobitism could be celebrated even by those who had benefitted from its destruction, and Vikki gets very excited, describing Charlie waiting at Glenfinnan, and thinking that no-one would rally to his cause:

'Suddenly the sound of the pipes aroused him, and he saw the clans coming down Glenfinnan. Soon after the MacDonalds appeared, and in the midst of a cheering host the Marquis of Tullibardine (Duke of Athole but for his attainder) unfurled the banner of King James.'

Commenting on the fact that 'poor Prince Charles' was a fugitive in the mountains hereabouts in 1746, she remarks that,

'I thought I never saw a lovelier or more romantic spot, or one which told its history so well. What a scene it must have been in 1745! And here was I, the descendant of the Stewarts and of the very king whom Prince Charles had sought to overthrow, sitting and walking about quite privately and peacefully.'

The monument is now in the care of the National Trust for Scotland, and open to the public.

A visit to MacDonald of Glenaladale who lived nearby brought out mementos of the '45; Charlie's snuff-mull, a watch and so forth, passed down in the family by the ancestor who aided Charles's attempt. Vikki comments, 'He is a Catholic, as are more of the people in this district.' Indeed, Catholicism and Jacobitism were almost synonymous in 1745. MacDonald took Brown and a couple of others up the monument, but Victoria declined when told 'the ascent was very awkward and difficult'. Imagine the consequences of Vikki getting her bulk stuck in the momument to Charles Edward! Especially when the paparazzi were lurking around, for on driving back the Queen commented, 'We met those dreadful reporters, including the man who behaved so ill on Saturday, as we were coming back.'

The next day, after leaving a few presents for her hosts, Lord and Lady Abinger, Victoria and party departed for Inverness, via the steamer on the Caledonian canal, of which she typically comments, 'The Caledonian Canal is a very wonderful piece of engineering, but travelling by it is very tedious' though she dutifully copies down in her diary an account of how the locks work 'from an account General Ponsonby wrote for me'. From the canal, they admire the sights: Ben Nevis in mist 'which we hear is very generally the case', the Well of the Seven heads at Loch Oich, Fort Augustus 'where there was a triumphal arch', and the 'fine old ruin of Castle Urquhart'. En route as ever she noted the mountains 'one conically shaped one called Ben Tigh which towers above the rest' at Invergarry, and the 'fine mountain of Mealfourvonie' which she estimates at 2,700ft high. It is actually much lower, but because of its fine shape and isolation, the Hill of the Cold Slopes was originally thought to be over 3,000ft.

They got off the steamer at Dochgarroch and entered 'a hired (not very beautiful) landau', and escorted by the 7th Dragoon Guards, entered Inverness to catch the train. Again, despite the fact that she was only there a few minutes, 'The streets were full of decorations and arches, and lined with volunteers... The fine-looking old Provost was there, and the Master of Lovat...' And so homeward, Vikki clearly having in her own mind squared all the circles concerned with Jacobitical romance and Hanoverian legitimacy. Her increasingly exalted ideas of monarchy were encouraged by Beaconsfield, and Vikki seems to have begun to believe that she actually ruled the country, saying she would 'never be a democratic monarch'. But this was an illusion, like her dreams of divinely ordained, royal descent. On one occasion she was talking to the Whig historian, Lord Macauley, and she referred to, 'My ancestor, Charles I' – who had been beheaded by Cromwell. Macauley's instant response was savage, but correct. 'You mean your Majesty's predecessor,' he replied since Vikki's claim to the throne was not by direct hereditary succession, but by parliamentary statute.

## A Tour in Campbell's Kingdom

There had always been a special relationship between the Campbells of Argyll, and the Hanoverian Monarchy. In 1715 the Campbells had defeated the Jacobite Army at Sheriffmuir, and in 1745 many of the clan fought against Prince Charles at Culloden. Honours were showered on the family, and when the Princess Louise married the Marquis of Lorne, the Campbell heir, it was the first time in over four centuries that a princess had, with royal consent, married outside the ruling house. Victoria had already visited Argyll in 1847 and 1871, and she renewed her aquaintance with Campbell's Kingdom in 1875, on a visit to her daughter and son-in-law.

Vikki took the train only as far as Tyndrum, as the extension to Oban was still under construction. There they were met by the Breadalbanes, the second most imprortant branch of the Campbell clan, and they continued their journey in the sociable. Victoria noted 'the lead mines belonging to Lord Breadalbane' at Tyndrum. The remains of the workings are still visible, and the old pony track gives a good walk up to the shafts. Victoria, however, was more interested in the country which became 'more and more beautiful' as they progressed, admiring Ben Lui and Ben Cruachan, before reaching Dalmally and taking the Inveraray road, whence they viewed the romantic ruins of Kilchurn Castle on Loch Awe. They drove through Glen Aray to the castle at Invereray, where the Duke and Duchess awaited, as well as 'halberdiers... posted in intervals along the approach, dressed in Campbell tartan kilts... with them were also the pipers of the volunteers.'

Next day the morning was spent in a wee stroll 'up the lower walk' of the wooded hill, Dunaquoich, which is prominent beside the castle, and on top of which is a tower. The afternoon was spent in repeating a drive which had been 'made' for Vikki on a previous visit in 1871, and now known as the Queen's Drive. This is a bit tricky to follow, but probably went up from the castle to *Lechkenvohr* [Leacan Mhor] and then down to *Carlonnan* before attaining the Dhu Loch at the foot of Glen Shire, up which the party rode a considerable distance. Of the Dhu Loch she noted it was 'a complete contrast to our Dhu Loch, for this was surrounded by green and very wooded hills...'. Not all Vikki's time was spent in sightseeing, for the next day there was a ball, which took place in a 'temporary pavillion'. Although enjoying the fun, Vikki was a bit nonplussed, and slightly disapproving, saying, 'It was not like the Highland balls I have been accustomed to, as there were many other dances besides reels. The band could not play reels (which were played by the piper), and yet came from Glasgow!' Did she imagine that the industrial proletarians of Clydeside spent their time dancing reels? She probably did. She had made a royal visit to Glasgow in 1849, and one of the things she records about it in her *Journal* was Rob Roy's visit to the cathedral in Scott's eponymous novel... an imaginary event.

The Campbells, due to their proximity to the Lowlands (especially Glasgow, with which they were closely connected), and their Hanoverian inclinations, had been early improving landlords. Long before the destruction of the old patriarchal Highland economy had begun in many places, on much of the Campbell lands it was almost completed, with tenures becoming commercial relationships, unlinked to military service. Ironically, a short distance from Inveraray Castle, there survived a couple of examples of the ancient form of land tenure as a museum piece which was of sufficient curiosity for the Duke to give Victoria an account of. After a rainy morning, it cleared in the late afternoon, and the Duke went for a drive with Vikki in the waggonette. They passed his deer park, and took the Lochgilphead road. They drove past some villages, including '...Achnagoul and Achindrain... old Highland villages, where a common old practice, now fallen into disuse, continues...'. The Duke wrote an account of the system for her, just as Ponsonby had written an account of the Caledonian Canal. On both occasions, she seemed little interested in actually going to observe these aspects of material production, being interested only in scenery. The Duke told her that,

'In the Highlands of Scotland up to a comparatively recent date the old system of village tenure prevailed as the common system of land tenure. Under this system the cultivators were collected into groups or villages... The farm itself was divided into pasture land and arable land. The pasture land was held in common by all the families, and the arable land was divided by lot every year... [This] has now almost entirely disappeared in the Highlands...'

In Achnagoul, in 1847, the tenants 'were persuaded with much difficulty to give up this old, semi-barbarous system and to divide the arable land into fixed divisions...', but the system appears to have continued longer in Achindrain, which is today a very interesting museum of Highland life. It is open to the public and well worth the trouble of inspecting. The Duke mentioned that the crofting system had replaced the old communal system of tenure, 'such crofters or very small cultivators as remain are generally separate from each other – each living on his own croft...'. Interestingly, we are on the verge of the crofters' agitation and the Crofters' War, which led to the Liberal government of Gladstone passing legislation to protect the small cultivators in the 1880s, after similarly passing the Irish Land Act of 1881. The Campbell family, Whigs and Liberals for generations, were fiercely opposed to these interferences in the rights of landed proprietors, and defected to the Tories, leading to a century of Campbellism and Conservatism in Argyll, only recently ended.

The mother-in-law's trip was nearing its end, but there was one last outing before the journey home. In the 18th century Rob Roy had played the double agent between the Jacobites and Hanoverians so fully that he himself probably forgot which side he was on. The Campbells did not really care, as Rob was the sworn enemy of the Duke of Montrose, in turn the Campbells' supreme hate; as long as Rob was prepared to harry and harass Montrose, he could find security on Campbell lands. In addition, Rob's wife was a Campbell, and clan blood was much thicker than water. So in the time of his greatest danger, Rob was able to seek refuge in Campbell's Kingdom, and lived at the head of Glen Shira, where Vikki noted 'are the remains of a house where Rob Roy lived for some time concealed, but on sufferance. His army or followers were hidden in Glen Shira.' They drove up Glen Shira to its head, passing the Dhu Loch, initially through a fine old avenue of beeches, and then into the glen itself. 'It is a lovely glen, wilder and much shut in as you advance, with fine rocks appearing through the grassy hills, and thickly wooded at the bottom.' They got out to look at some falls on the river Shira, then drove further to picnic and paint.

On 29 September they headed for home, by a different route from the outward journey. Leaving Inveraray they changed horses at the inn at Cairndow, and ascended the steep road to 'the very wild and desolate Glenkinglass', where despite the addition of a pair of leaders, the horses almost failed to carry the party to the summit. At the summit, Vikki noticed 'an inscription cut upon a stone by the regiment which made the road, which was one of the military roads to open up the Highlands constructed by Government under the superintendence of Marshall Wade. The stone remains, but the words are much defaced.' In a mixture of sunshine and showers, they crossed Glen Croe, 'something like Glencoe, but not so fine and the road much steeper', after which were rewarding glimpses of Ben Lomond and 'the celebrated Cobbler, or Ben Arthur'.

The drive down Loch Lomondside was, as it always is, splendid, and at Luss an old woman gave Vikki a bag of 'sweeties'. At

Rossdhu there is the usual guard of Highland volunteers, drawn up by Colquhoun of Luss, and finally they reached Balloch where the train took them to Stirling and then to Ballater via Aberdeen, and home to Balmoral. Having resided a few days at Campbell's Kingdom, she was now back in her own.

### WALK 21: ROB ROY'S HOUSE (Map A)
### 11 miles, 4 – 6 hours

*A walk based on this tour would be to follow Victoria's trip in Glen Shira. It is possible to walk up the eastern side of the glen on the land-rover track, past the appropriately named Maam, to eventually arrive at the site of Rob Roy's house, which is marked on the* OS *map. There is now a hydro-electric scheme in the glen, and whether you will see Vikki's waterfalls in all their glory depends partly on the workings of the Shira Dam. Coming back down to a bridge at Drimlee, it is possible to cross, and return by the west bank of the River Shira to the Dubh Loch. (*OS *56)*

# The Wild West Tour

Victoria's last big outing took her further north and west in the Highlands than she had ever been before, to Loch Maree and Torridon. Indeed, Wester Ross in 1877 was still far of the tourist circuit, though improving communications and maps were beginning to change this. However, this was still the real Highlands, dominated by crofting, the Gaelic language and Free Kirkism, which Deeside was not. On 12 September, the route of 1872 was repeated as far as Dingwall, Vikki noticing that the corn was cut early near Aberdeen, though harvesting was still going on further north. She also noted 'the heather beautiful everywhere'.

At Dingwall they were met by Mackenzie of Gairloch and his wife, who have 'an immense property about here, and all around is Mackenzie country'. The construction of the railway line towards Kyle allowed the party to continue by rail to Achnasheen, passing 'Strathpeffer, which is extremely pretty... a wooded glen with houses and cottages dotted about...'. Achnasheen was described as 'only a small station and two or three little cottages' – but even here 'there were Gaelic inscriptions, and some plaids arranged in festoons'. The sociable took them onwards to Loch Maree 'through a desolate, wild and perfectly uninhabited country'. Always one for noting peaks, she comments, 'Looking back you see the three high peaks of *Scour-na-Vuillin* [Sgurr a' Mhuillin]'. After changing horses at Kinlochewe, they carried on ten miles to 'the hotel of Loch Maree' at Talladale.

Loch Lomond and Loch Maree vie in most people's opinion as the most beautiful loch in the Highlands, and Victoria exults over the scenery: 'The drive along the lochside... is beautiful in the extreme. The hills to the right, as you go from Kinlochewe, are splendid – very high and serrated, with woods at the base of them.' As she drove through the scene of loch, mountain, pines and islands, she was additionally rewarded with the sight of a rainbow. After one of the showers, the sky turned crimson and 'lit up *Ben Sleach*' [Slioch]. She was especially pleased that her 'dear little sitting room' at the hotel had a view of the mountain. Vikki was always keen to get the names of the hills, as an event next day showed. Going out for a short walk they came across 'a cottage, a miserable hovel, in which an old man lived... [who] said he 'had very little English', which is the case with most people here.' Brown was told to give him something, and ask the names of the local hills.

A couple of days later, they decided to visit Torridon 'described as fine and wild', although the weather was unpromising. After midday they started off in the wagonette, and the day turned fine with only a few showers. Passing the Bridge of Grudie, 'a very pretty rapid burn, with fine fir trees', 'Ben Sleach' was once again admired, but they ain't seen nothing yet. Changing horses at Kinlochewe, they turned towards Torridon, 'mountains towering up, as we advanced, like mighty giants'. They reached *Loch Clare* [Clair] and marvelled; the Cairngorms had not prepared them for this!

'Soon after this the grand, wild, savage-looking, but most picturesque Glen of Torridon opened upon us, with the dark mural precipices of that most extraordinary mountain *Ben Liughach* [Liatach], which the people pronounce Liarach. We were quite amazed as we drove below it. The mountains here rise so abruptly from their base that they seem much higher than our Aberdeenshire mountains... All the hills about Loch Maree and this glen, and elsewhere in this neighbourhood, are very serrated and rocky. Ben Liarach is most peculiar from its being so dark, and the rocks like terraces one above the other, or like fortifications and pillars....'

At Upper Loch Torridon the Skye hills were seen, and a secluded spot was found for lunch and sketching in the 'delicious' air of the mountains and the sea. The spot was probably in the vicinity of Lower Diabeg. But there is a dark side to this idyllic outing: the poverty of the local people. Victoria describes that 'on the slope of a hill, was a row of five or six wretched hovels, before which stood bare-legged and very ill-clad children, and poor women literally squatting on the ground.' Later on the trip she met 'three of four poorly dressed bairns', and gave them their left-over sandwiches and biscuits. She also remarked again that hardly anyone here could speak English, and they had trouble getting an interpreter in the local 'shoppie' where Vikki bought some trifles. This monolingualism was soon to change however. The 1872 Education Act had provided for the introduction of elementary schooling everywhere. Victoria mentions that 'There was a school, standing detached by itself, which had been lately built.' Instruction would be in English, and soon lead to the erosion of Gaelic monolingualism in the area, as in others.

The following day was the Sabbath, and this area was heavily influenced by Free Kirk sabbatarianism. Victoria was impressed by the fact that, though there was no kirk nearer than Kinlochewe or Gairloch, 'people had been seen passing on foot as early as half past seven to Gairloch'. She herself had taken a short walk in the morning, again finding that in a local cottage, the inhabitant, a Mrs Macrae 'could hardly understand or speak a word of

English'. Again, her cottage was described as 'very poor looking' and 'wet and muddy almost to the door'. Though Vikki said her prayers privately that day, I'm sure Mrs Macrae and others would not have approved of her taking a morning walk merely for pleasure, and certainly would have disapproved of the journey she took in the afternoon to visit the islands of Loch Maree.

Their landlord at the hotel, a Mr Hornsby, was obviously not a local, and was prepared to provide the royals with a boat, and to row them himself – the dictates of tourism eroding sabbatarianism already! The day was calm, and a delightful row was had through the wooded islands on the blue waters of the loch, with Slioch towering over them. They disembarked on the Isle of Maree (*Eilan Maree*), and visited the sites. Scrambling through the dense undergrowth, they first visited a well whose waters were said to be a cure for insanity, 'now nearly dry'. Nearby was an old tree, where visitors hammered offerings to Saint Maelrubha into the bark, and Vikki 'hammered some pennies into the tree', noting that rags and ribbons were also tied to its branches. Despite sabbatarianism, some primitive superstitions clearly survived in the area. The island had been the site of an old monastery, whose ruins were examined, and also boasted some interesting old gravestones. Two belonged to a Norwegian or Danish princess, though Vikki noted that the most recent burial was only eight years previously. Never one to hang about, Vikki observed of this trip: 'It took about twenty minutes.' They rowed back to the shore, had tea, and took in a scramble to a waterfall 'very inferior to those in our neighbourhood at Balmoral', before returning to the hotel, and spending the evening reading and writing.

The following day a strange incident took place. Victoria had heard that some people had 'asked permission to come over from Stornoway' expressly to see 'their beloved Queen', and she decided to go towards Gairloch to meet them, which she did at Kerrie's Bridge near Charlestown. Here, with their minister, the Lewis people – 250 of them – sang 'God Save the Queen', which Vikki found 'very gratifying', as indeed she would. But was this a genuine expression of monarchical fervour? Victoria lets slip that she had already seen the 'many fishermen amongst them' on the previous Saturday, 'coming back from having sold their fish'. In other words, they had come over to Gairloch to engage in trade, had been disinclined to travel on the Sunday as strict sabbatarians and had hung around on the Monday to see Vikki – quite a different scenario from the one she had been presented with of the Lewis people asking permission to come across for the sole purpose of seeing her! And even this hanging around... I wonder how much their landlord, Matheson, who was in the vicinity, had to do with this through his influence on the minister who had accompanied the people?

Wasps had been a problem on this trip, and gauze was nailed down on the hotel windows to keep them out. No such simple solution to the problem of the midges offered itself, however. 'The midges are dreadful, and you cannot stand for a moment without being stung.'

The return homewards was uneventful, and the weather bad which obscured any view. At Achnasheen they were met by Alexander Matheson, MP and chairman of the railway company. Matheson, having made his fortune in the drug trade between India and China, had bought Lewis with part of the profits; in the process he attempted to turn Lewis into a private feudal kingdom, along the lines of Balmoral. Doubtless Vikki, who took various drugs herself, would not have seen his wealth as immoral earnings, or its use as retrograde.

The Wild West Tour was the last of Vikki's Highland trips.

# Balmorality No More?

The trip with Eugenie to the Gelder Shiel in 1879 was Victoria's last entry in her *Journal*. The first event of major significance after this was the death of John Brown in 1883, which allowed Vikki to resume the mantle of mourning which she felt became her so well. He died of complications arising from a chill – which it was rumoured had been caused by a drunken chase after phantom Fenians – and was laid in virtual state in Baille-na-Coille, a house Vikki had had built for him. She wrote that she was 'trying hard to occupy herself, but she is utterly crushed, and her life has again sustained one of those shocks like '61... and at every moment the loss of the strong arm... is most cruelly missed.' Broon was buried in Crathie Kirkyard, and Vikki's message on his tombstone went 'Well done, good and faithful servant... I will make thee ruler over many things' – and indeed she had. Her favour had allowed Brown to become a downstairs tyrant and an upstairs boor, without fear of reprimand. But this Malvolio was a pathetic character, his ambitions circumscribed by his limited intelligence to those of the besotted bully... or possibly not; possibly even Brown realised that if his ambitions were not curtailed to petty things, even Victoria could not save him from the mass of envy and resentment he generated. At any rate he ended up a rich man, for as well as his house and various possessions which came as gifts, Brown was worth £7,000 when he died, a vast fortune for a Deeside peasant at that time – or even for a middle-class person. (A minimum factor of 50 in multiplication would give today's value of that sum.)

Victoria shocked many by erecting a life-size statue, by Boehm, to Brown at Balmoral, giving him thus the same treatment as Albert. On it the Poet Laureate, Tennyson, wrote the lines,

Friend more than servant, loyal, truthful, brave
Self less than duty, even to the grave.

Victoria also decided to work on the second volume of her *Highland Journal*, and to dedicate it to Brown, as the first had been dedicated to Albert. Its Preface stated, 'To my loyal Highlanders, and especially to the memory of my devoted Personal Attendant and faithful friend, John Brown, These records of my widowed life in Scotland are gratefully dedicated, Victoria R.I.' Indeed, Vikki contemplated a third volume, dedicated to the Life of Broon himself, and only the horrified reaction of Ponsonby, her private secretary, and the Dean of Windsor persuaded her to desist. Apparently the manuscript was drafted, but destroyed by Ponsonby; there are also rumours of the existence of a diary by Brown himself, again either destroyed or lost. So one has to ask: what was in them that might have sullied the reputation of the monarchy?

After this, almost two decades were to elapse before Victoria's death in 1901. At Balmoral she passed them in a diminishing round of rituals and activities. More statues were erected, one of Victoria herself by Bertie in 1887. Strolling players came to entertain – the D'Oyly Carte came to do the *Mikado* – and there were activities like the gillies' ball to pass the time. Trips were shorter, to the old women to distribute royal largesse, or for tea to the Dantzig Shiel, so called because a German once had a sawmill there. Foreign heads of state were entertained, like the Tsar of Russia, who witnessed bonfires on the Deeside hills and heard massed pipers on his way from Ballater to Balmoral. Vikki was Jingoist to the last, giving her royal blessing to the futile carnage of the Boer War at the end of her reign, as she had done to that in Crimea near its beginning. The relief of Mafeking especially lifted her spirits. But in November 1900 she left Balmoral for Windsor, visiting her loyal old ladies with the message, 'I have come to say good-bye to you, and I hope you will have a comfortable winter, and keep well till I come back.' She died, however, on 22 January 1901.

A century after her death, Victoria's legacy still dominates Deeside. The emblems and icons of monarchy are everywhere, in the villages, on the estates, and even in the hills themselves. Additionally, though now surpassed by mountaineering as a draw, many visitors still come to Deeside for its associations with royalty. (After the film, you can now take a bus tour from Aberdeen called

'The Mrs Brown Experience' – what does it consist of? Lying back and thinking of Billy Connolly?) More than any other part of Scotland, Upper Deeside still probably looks closer to what it looked a century ago, the granite, timber and corrugated iron constructions of Braemar giving it a Sleepy Hollow appearance. The Big Hooses of the Victorian gentry are still there, and land usage is still overwhelmingly dominated by deer forest – at least was, until the recent acquisition of the Mar estate by the National Trust. But things do change even on the Brae o Mar, which is possibly Scotland's Mecklenburg. Bismarck remarked that when the end of the world came he would like to be in Mecklenburg, since everything there happened half a century late. And even beneath the pageantry of the latter half of the 19th century, society slowly changed on Deeside even if the landscape did not.

Ironically, given its advertisement as the official, 'Royal Highlands', by the time of Victoria's death there was almost nothing Highland about Deeside, apart from the scenery and the place names. Gaelic, the main stamp of Highland culture, had been struggling even when Victoria came to Deeside in 1848, and by 1900 it was virtually extinct east of Braemar, and even there used only in the home. Doric, the Scots patois of the North-East, was dominant. Crofting was another mark of the Highland community at this time, but apart from pockets of tenure at Inverey and Glengairn, there were almost no crofters on Deeside, certainly by 1900. It was this fact, gained from his personal residences on Deeside, which caused Gladstone to exclude the area from the Crofters Acts of the 1880s. Deeside was deer forest with a few farms, not crofting territory.

A related point is the influence of the Free Kirk, which became a mark of much of Highland society at this time. Whilst the Free Kirk had a presence in rural Aberdeenshire, and places of worship at Ballater and Crathie, it never assumed the dominance it did in the crofting areas, whose population formed its backbone in an anti-landlord protest. This in turn meant that the dominant politics of the Deeside area became Conservative, against the Liberal politics which marked the crofting Western Highlands; gamekeepers

**John Brown's Body (1870) from W & D Downey of London**
(Aberdeen Art Gallery and Museums)
The man in his Highland regalia, photographed by Downey in the 1870s. His unimaginative
arrogance comes through well here. Though they did not, and never had, dressed like this, this
was the High Victorian image of a loyal Highland peasant.

**Charles Edward Stuart (1888) by George Washington Wilson**
(Aberdeen Art Gallery and Museums)

If you think virtual reality was invented in the 1990s, think again. A hundred years before that, the Victorians staged extensive – and expensive – tableaux vivants, where they re-enacted the past. Here we have Princess Victoria as Flora MacDonald and Prince Albert Victor as the fugitive Bonnie Prince Charlie, guarded by loyal Highlanders. The Hanoverians appropriating Stuart sentimentality.

**Malcolm Canmore (1888) by George Washington Wilson**
(Aberdeen Art Gallery and Museums)

Victoria's attempt to legitimise herself by seeking a direct link with the Stuarts we have discussed. Less well known is the projection of this back to the early days of the Scottish Monarchy, when Malcolm Canmore, the first Deeside royal resident, and his English Queen Margaret ruled. Princess Beatrice plays the Saint Queen, and Prince Henry, Malcolm Canmore.

**The Queen's Bedroom at Balmoral (1865) by George Wilson**
(Aberdeen Art Gallery and Museums)

Washington Wilson must have been one of the few men given access to this room after Albert's death. Here we have the heavy Victorian iconography of family and death (note the wreath, and Albert picture above the bed) combined with ubiquitous tartan, and images of the Highlands above the mantelpiece. If Broon entered this chamber, he was a brave man in my opinion.

and fermers tend to be Tories, not Liberals. The population of Deeside was thirled to a neo-feudality, whose social peace made it very attractive for the urban bourgeoisie, themselves gradually moving from liberalism to conservatism in the face of the threat supposedly posed by the working class, and the rise of imperialism. Downstream from Balmoral, James 'Paraffin' Young was to buy Durris House, while the Coates family, of Paisley thread-mill fame, acquired Glentanar. The local population may not have been radical, but they had a pawky sense of humour: Durris was named Paraffin Ha', while Glentanar became Pirn Ha'.

I have given voice to those who raised theirs in criticism of the doings of the monarchy, on Deeside and elsewhere, during Victoria's reign, and do not intend to stop now. Despite the Jubilee, 1887 had been quite a bad year for Vikki. As well as the Trafalgar Square Riots, Charles Bradlaugh the radical and atheist MP was suggesting that Buckingham Palace be turned into a home for fallen women, while the ever irritant Dilkes was saying the monarchy was giving little value for its £1,000,000 a year and should be abolished. Vikki was furious that Gladstone ignored these attacks, insisting that non-rebuttal meant that 'these revolutionary theories are allowed to produce what effect they may in the minds of the working classes'. But the surge of prosperity and imperialist patriotism from 1890 meant that criticism of the monarchy abated till after Victoria's death.

In the social and political conditions of the 1930s radical republican sentiment revived, and George Scott-Moncrieff coined the term *Balmorality* to describe what had happened to Scotland in the 19th century, arguing that Victoria should bear prime responsibility for the production of a trashy version of Highland life, and its extension to epitomise Scotland as a whole. He criticised 'the deadening slime of Balmorality, a glutinous compound of hypocrisy, false sentiment, industrialism, ugliness and clammy pseudo-Calvinism'. Twenty years later Ivor Brown would defend Vikki saying that she might have been the indirect cause of what Moncrieff describes, but 'an indirect cause is no proper recipient of censure for accidental results' and reminding us that, 'The way of the eminent among the ordinary is always difficult'. And indeed, a proper understanding allows us to see Vikki as a catalyst who speeded up a process already underway through the interpretation put on Scott by the wider Victorian public, and stimulated by the Highlander as Praetorian Guard of British Imperialism.

And what of today? The last couple of decades have seen the monarchy involved in struggles with paparazzi anxious for details about the latest family or sexual scandal, and criticisms of the expense of the monarchy and calls for its reform or abolition as an undemocratic institution. The reader will have discovered that in one sense, all this is nothing new, as these features were familiar a century ago in the Balmoral soap opera. But we live in a different world in 2000 from 1900, one where many of the apparently imperishable monarchies which existed in Victoria's time have vanished, and where constitutional change is underway in Britain itself, with Scottish and Welsh devolution and abolition of the House of Lords. Our Australian cousins only failed to abolish the monarchy because the republican cause was split over what is to replace it. Everyone knows that next time they will. Looking at the Chookie Embro making racist remarks around the world, or Bonnie Prince Charlie with his superannuated dreams of a neo-feudal Britain, we should ask ourselves, do we really need this? My auld grannie used to say she didn't want to be queen because 'her life isn't her own'. There is a simple solution to that – abolish the monarchy and given them back their life. The greatest compliment I can pay Vikki, having followed her across Scotland, is that, of them all, she might actually have enjoyed aspects of such a restitution of her existence. Mrs Brown was the best of the bunch, but nevertheless the best of a bad lot.

The image that will remain with me after writing this book, is that of the 656 horses it required to take the Royal party to Breadalbane in 1842, for a piece of neo-feudal nonsense... 656 horses. The Highlands were starving, and in the Glasgow slums people slept a dozen or more to a room... and 656 horses were employed taking Victoria to Taymouth; 656 horses which were undoubtedly better fed than the population of the Highlands, and better housed than the inhabitants of the Glasgow slums. Anyone who feels that was reasonable or rational, then or now, is either an escapee from a mental institution, or a candidate for one. Remember those horses, as you walk in the footsteps of Queen Victoria.

# BIBLIOGRAPHY

THERE IS A SPLENDID, stoutly monarchist and lavishly illustrated version of *Queen Victoria's Highland Journals*, edited by David Duff, first published in 1980, the latest edition with a *Mrs Brown* film cover. Copies of *Leaves from the Journal of Our Life in the Highlands*, in the first (1868) edition with the original illustrations, can still be got unaccountably quite cheap in second hand bookshops, though possibly not for much longer. My own was bought in 1869 by a Mary Cargill. John Kerr has edited a volume of Victoria's writings dealing with Perthshire, which is as lavishly illustrated and as sycophantically uncritical as is Duff's volume. It is entitled, rather inaccurately given its geographical bias, *Queen Victoria's Scottish Diaries* (1992). Duff and Kerr are often available remaindered, which may say something about the current state of the monarchy.

Biographies of Victoria are legion; a vast opus is that of Stanley Weintraub, *Victoria: Biography of a Queen* (1987); it is heavy going, but useful if you like the intricacies of royal lineages, and details of what Vikki ate and wore. Weintraub also wrote a biography of Albert, which strikes me as a major feat of the imagination. For non-monarchists wanting a wee summary of Victoria's life, the recent *Queen Victoria*, by Elizabeth Longford (1999) would probably suffice. On the Deeside residency, *Balmoral: The History of a Home* (1955) by Ivor Brown gives us monarchist Scotland at its best – or worst. Fenton Wyness' *Royal Valley: the Aberdeenshire Dee* (1968) is similarly uncritical though less mawkish in its treatment of the monarchy, and is a storehouse of well-researched material on the history of the region. Brown and Wyness are currently out of print, but often available second hand.

Two books by Robert Smith deserve special mention. Firstly his *Grampian Ways* (1980) which has much detail on the old Mounth roads, many of which Victoria travelled, but more especially his lovely, heart-rending *Land of the Lost* (1997) which unearths a wealth of detail about the vanished townships of the

Aberdeenshire Highlands, and which has a fine, critical edge sadly lacking in most of the obsequious accounts of the history and culture of Deeside. A section of my own *Scotland's Mountains before the Mountaineers* (1998) called 'The Cairngorms before the Climbers' deals with the exploration of Deeside by such as mapmakers, geologists, hunters and artists, from the beginnings up to the Victorian period. The film, *Mrs Brown*, is also worth seeing, despite the odd piece of dramatic licence and innacuracy. The performances of Judi Dench as Vikki and Billy Connolly as Billy Connolly are magnificent.

# PLACES TO VISIT

IF THE WEATHER FORBIDS outdoor trips, or simply if time allows, the following places are open to visitors. Contact beforehand as admission times/charges are liable to alter. Places easily accessible by public transport indicated.

## On Donside/Deeside

(Further information from Aberdeen and Grampian Tourist Board, 27 Albyn Place, Aberdeen AB10 1YL, Tel 01224 288 800.) Places accessible from Aberdeen-Braemar bus route indicated with *.

**Balmoral Castle**: grounds and part of residence now open to visitors when family not there. Statues of Vikki, Broon, Albert... if you like that sort of thing. Expensive. (Tel 01339 742 334) * MAPS E,F,G.

**Braemar Castle**: built c1625 by Earl of Mar, later passed to, and still held by Farquharsons. Relics of family, Jacobitism etc. Dungeon and iron yett. Garrisoned 1745-1831. (Tel 01339 741 219) * MAP I.

**Braemar Graveyard**: graves of Maggie Gruer, Patrick Grant (Dubrach), Farquharsons. Always open. * MAP I.

**Ballater Station**: fine intact example of Deeside railway architecture; railway memorabilia and tea-room. * MAP H.

**Corgarff Castle**: (Historic Scotland) fortified house, burnt in 16th century Forbes/Gordon feud. Extended post 1745 (star curtain wall) against Jacobites and smugglers. Exhibition. (Tel 0131 668 8800) MAP F.

**Crathie Kirk**: John Brown's body lies a mouldering in his grave here. * MAP E.

**Invercauld Arms,** Braemar: Site (inside hotel) of Raising of Standard in 1715. * MAP G.

**Kindrochit Castle,** Braemar: (Historic Scotland) ruins of original castle, 14th century till c1600, by Cluanie Water. Always open – no roof! * MAP G.

**Lecht Lead Mine:** worth a wee stroll from the road. Engine room standing. At nearby Well of Lecht is a memorial stone to 33rd Regiment who built road to the Spey in 1745. MAP F.

**Lochnagar Distillery,** Crathie: still producing the craitur and a fine one at that. Vikki visited in 1848, and so can you. (Tel 01339 742 273) * MAP E.

**Mar Lodge,** opposite Inverey: now National Trust for Scotland holiday flats, occasionally open to public. Built 1890s, relics of Vikki, Duffs. Ballroom adjacent to Lodge is roofed with thousands of antlers. (Contact NTS at Tel 0131 226 5922 for information.) MAP I.

**Our Lady of the Snows:** wonderfully named chapel at Corgarff; details of life of Catholic pocket of west Aberdeenshire. Indwelling caretaker. MAP F.

**Pannanich Wells Inn,** West of Ballater: site of former mineral spa. Now producing mineral water again. MAP H.

## Elsewhere in Scotland

**Abbotsford,** 2 miles west of Melrose: home of Walter Scott, expresses architecture of his mind. Built 1820s, packed with memorabilia. (Tel 01896 822 043) MAP J.

**Ardoch Roman Camp,** Braco: (Historic Scotland) astonishing earthwork encampment, mainly second century. Vikki didn't get out of her carriage to see it; you should. Always open. MAP A.

**Auchindrayne Township,** south of Inveraray: History/artefacts of the last communal clachan. Several period buildings remain. (Tel 01499 500 235) MAP A.

**Blair Castle,** Blair Atholl: history of family, Atholl Highlanders armoury etc. Jacobite interest – Claverhouse buried in Old Blair Kirkyard (1689) after Battle of Killiekrankie. Castle besieged by Jacobites in 1746. (Tel 01796 481 207) Blair Atholl Station. MAP G.

**Banavie Locks,** near Fort William: Neptune's Staircase on Caledonian Canal (opened 1822) still in use. Watch the ships pass. Thomas Telford's masterpiece. Corrach Station. MAP D.

**Dryburgh Abbey:** (Historic Scotland) though Vikki only 'caught a glimpse' of it, worth visiting for Walter Scott tomb. 12th/13th century edifice, destroyed by English, the Reformation got the blame. (Tel 0131 668 8800) MAP J.

**Dumbarton Castle:** (Historic Scotland) tremendous situation, historical associations, Wallace, Mary Queen of Scots. (Tel 0131 668 8800) Dumbarton East Station. MAP C.

**Dunkeld** Cathedral: (Historic Scotland Tel 0131 668 8800). Originally Celtic institution, this one was damaged in the Reformation. Suffered further in 1689. Col Cleland, Cameronian leader, buried inside. (Tel 0131 668 8800)
Town: much rebuilt after 1689, 'little houses' later restored by National Trust for Scotland – headquarters in Ell House in town. Details of **Hermitage** (NTS) from same place. (Tel 01350 727 460) Dunkeld Station. MAP B.

**Dunrobin Castle,** Golspie: I do not intend to visit till the last Duchess of Sutherland is strangled in the entrails of the last sheep. But you can if you want. (Tel 01408 633 177) MAP B.

**Fingal's Cave,** Staffa. (NTS) Discovered by Banks 1772, visited by everybody famous. (Contact 0141 616 2266 for details of landings etc.) MAP C.

**Floors Castle,** Kelso: Adam mansion, added to 1840s. (Tel 01573 223 333) MAP J.

**Fortingall,** nr. Aberfeldy: ancient yew tree in kirkyard, also Celtic Christian relics in kirk. Earthworks of once-thought Roman camp west of village. MAP A.

**Glenfinnan Monument:** (NTS) Jacobite standard erected 18 August 1745, monument erected 1815. (Tel 01397 722 250) Glenfinnan Station. MAP D.

**Hermitage:** near Dunkeld (see Dunkeld) MAP B.

**Iona and Abbey:** (NTS) Relics of Celtic Christianising of Scotland, Saint Columba etc. Ferry (no cars) from Fionnphort, Mull. (Tel 0141 616 2266) MAP C.

**Inveraray Castle:** Campbell château – artefacts of the most powerful Highland clan. The 18th century planned town is also worth a visit, especially the historic courthouse and jail. (Tel 01499 302 381) MAP A.

**Loch of the Lowes,** east of Dunkeld: Scottish Wildlife Trust reserve, woodland walks, bird hides (chance of seeing ospreys). (Tel 01350 727 337) MAP B.

**Melrose Abbey:** (Historic Scotland) Ruins of 12th century institution. Contains Bruce's heart. Again, Reformers got the blame for English destruction. (Tel 0131 668 8800) MAP J.

**Ruthven Barracks,** near Kingussie: (Historic Scotland) built after 1715 Rebellion on former Comyn motte. Extended by Wade 1734. Garrison surrendered to Jacobites 1746. (Tel 0131 668 8800) Kingussie Station. MAP G.

**Smailholm Tower,** near Melrose: (Historic Scotland) 16th century Border tower. Walter Scott associations. (Tel 0131 668 8800) MAP J.

**Trossachs Pier:** *ss Walter Scott* summer sailings on Loch Katrine on 1900 steamer. (Tel 0141 336 5333 or 955 0128) MAP A.

**_Waverley_ Excursions:** Anderston Quay, Glasgow. Summer sailings to Loch Long, Kyles of Bute etc. Historic ocean-going paddle steamer (1947). (Tel 0141 221 8152) Anderston Station MAP E.

# CHRONOLOGY

| | |
|---|---|
| 1819 | Victoria born. |
| | 'Peterloo' Massacre of trades union demonstrators, Manchester. |
| 1822 | Walter Scott organises visit of George IV to Edinburgh; start of 'tartanism'. |
| 1832 | Reform Act enfranchises much of middle-class Britain. |
| 1837 | Victoria ascends Throne. |
| 1840 | Victoria marries Albert. |
| 1842 | First visit to Scotland. |
| | 'Plug Riots' during Chartist attempted General Strike. |
| 1848 | Takes lease on Balmoral. |
| | Revolt in Ireland. |
| | 'Year of Revolutions' in Europe. |
| 1850s | Knoydart Clearances. |
| 1851 | Great Exhibition opened. |
| | Britain 'Workshop of the World'. |
| 1853 | Crimean War starts. |
| 1854 | Balmoral completed; 'Balmorality' begins. |
| 1861 | Albert dies. |
| 1860s | Mourning becomes Vikki. |
| 1867 | Second Reform Act; votes for skilled workers. |
| | *Capital* by Marx published. |
| 1868 | *Leaves from the Journal...* published. |
| 1870-1 | Franco-Prussian War. |
| | German Unification. |
| | France becomes a Republic. |
| 1870s | Rise of Republican sentiment. |
| 1872 | Vikki emerges from closet. |
| 1876 | Vikki Empress of India. |
| 1880s | Beginnings of mass Trades Unionism. |
| | 'Scramble for Africa'. |
| | Crofters' War. |
| 1883 | Broon shuffles off mortals. |
| 1884 | *More leaves...* published. |
| 1887 | Golden Jubilee. |
| | Trafalgar Square Riots. |
| 1888 | Vikki's daughter German Empress (for three months.) |
| 1890s | Imperialist conflicts in Africa/Asia. |
| 1897 | Diamond Jubilee. |
| 1898 | Boer War begins. |
| 1900 | Formation of Labour Representation Committee (soon to be the Labour Party). |
| 1901 | Victoria dies. |

# Some other books published by **LUATH** PRESS

## WALK WITH LUATH

### Scotland's Mountains before the Mountaineers

Ian Mitchell

ISBN 0 946487 39 1  PBK £9.99

In this ground-breaking book, Ian Mitchell tells the story of explorations and ascents in the Scottish Highlands in the days before mountaineering became a popular sport – when bandits, Jacobites, poachers and illicit distillers traditionally used the mountains as sanctuary. The book also gives a detailed account of the map makers, road builders, geologists, astronomers and naturalists, many of whom ascended hitherto untrodden summits while working in the Scottish Highlands.

*Scotland's Mountains before the Mountaineers* is divided into four Highland regions, with a map of each region showing key summits. While not designed primarily as a guide, it will be a useful handbook for walkers and climbers. Based on a wealth of new research, this book offers a fresh perspective that will fascinate climbers and mountaineers and everyone interested in the history of mountaineering, cartography, the evolution of landscape and the social history of the Scottish Highlands.

'... will give you much to think about next time you're up that mountain.' THE GUARDIAN

'To have produced a work of such significance that is also fun to read is an achievement.' HIGH

### Mountain Days & Bothy Nights

Dave Brown and Ian Mitchell

ISBN 0 946487 15 4  PBK £7.50

Acknowledged as a classic of mountain writing still in demand ten years after its first publication, this book takes you into the bothies, howffs and dosses on the Scottish hills. Fishgut Mac, Desperate Dan and Stumpy the Big Yin stalk hill and public house, evading gamekeepers and Royalty with a camaraderie which was the trademark of Scots hillwalking in the early days.

'The fun element comes through... how innocent the social polemic seems in our nastier world of today... the book for the rucksack this year.'
Hamish Brown,
SCOTTISH MOUNTAINEERING CLUB JOURNAL

### The Joy of Hillwalking

Ralph Storer

ISBN 0 946487 28 6  PBK £7.50

Apart, perhaps, from the joy of sex, the joy of hillwalking brings more pleasure to more people than any other form of human activity.

'Alps, America, Scandinavia, you name it – Storer's been there, so why the hell shouldn't he bring all these various and varied places into his observations... [He] even admits to losing his virginity after a day on the Aggy Ridge... Well worth its place alongside Storer's earlier works.'* TAC

## LUATH WALKING GUIDES

The highly respected and continually updated guides to the Cairngorms.

'Particularly good on local wildlife and how to see it'
THE COUNTRYMAN

### Walks in the Cairngorms

Ernest Cross

ISBN 0 946487 09 X  PBK £4.95

This selection of walks celebrates the rare birds, animals, plants and geological wonders of a region often believed difficult to penetrate on foot. Nothing is difficult with this guide in your pocket, as Cross gives a choice for every walker, and includes valuable tips on mountain safety and weather advice.

Ideal for walkers of all ages and skiers waiting for snowier skies.

### Short Walks in the Cairngorms

Ernest Cross

ISBN 0 946487 23 5  PBK £4.95

Cross wrote this volume after overhearing a walker remark that there were no short walks for lazy ramblers in the Cairngorm region. Here is the answer: rambles through scenic woods with a welcoming pub at the end, birdwatching hints, glacier holes, or for the fit and ambitious, scrambles up hills to admire vistas of glorious scenery. Wildlife in the Cairngorms is unequalled elsewhere in Britain, and here it is brought to the binoculars of any walker who treads quietly and with respect.

# ON THE TRAIL OF

## On the Trail of William Wallace

David R. Ross

ISBN 0 946487 47 2 PBK £7.99

How close to reality was *Braveheart*?

Where was Wallace actually born?

What was the relationship between Wallace and Bruce?

Are there any surviving eye-witness accounts of Wallace?

How does Wallace influence the psyche of today's Scots?

*On the Trail of William Wallace* offers a refreshing insight into the life and heritage of the great Scots hero whose proud story is at the very heart of what it means to be Scottish. Not concentrating simply on the hard historical facts of Wallace's life, the book also takes into account the real significance of Wallace and his effect on the ordinary Scot through the ages, manifested in the many sites where his memory is marked.

In trying to piece together the jigsaw of the reality of Wallace's life, David Ross weaves a subtle flow of new information with his own observations. His engaging, thoughtful and at times amusing narrative reads with the ease of a historical novel, complete with all the intrigue, treachery and romance required to hold the attention of the casual reader and still entice the more knowledgable historian.

    74 places to visit in Scotland and the north of England

    One general map and 3 location maps

    Stirling and Falkirk battle plans

    Wallace's route through London

    Chapter on Wallace connections in North America and elsewhere

    Reproductions of rarely seen illustrations

*On the Trail of William Wallace* will be enjoyed by anyone with an interest in Scotland, from the passing tourist to the most fervent nationalist. It is an encyclopaedia-cum-guide book, literally stuffed with fascinating titbits not usually on offer in the conventional history book.

David Ross is organiser of and historical adviser to the Society of William Wallace.

'*Historians seem to think all there is to be known about Wallace has already been uncovered. Mr Ross has proved that Wallace studies are in fact in their infancy.*' ELSPETH KING, Director the the Stirling Smith Art Museum & Gallery, who annotated and introduced the recent Luath edition of *Blind Harry's Wallace*.

'*Better the pen than the sword!*'

RANDALL WALLACE, author of *Braveheart*, when asked by David Ross how it felt to be partly responsible for the freedom of a nation following the Devolution Referendum.

## On the Trail of Robert the Bruce

David R. Ross

ISBN 0 946487 52 9 PBK £7.99

*On the Trail of Robert the Bruce* charts the story of Scotland's hero-king from his boyhood, through his days of indecision as Scotland suffered under the English yoke, to his assumption of the crown exactly six months after the death of William Wallace. Here is the astonishing blow by blow account of how, against fearful odds, Bruce led the Scots to win their greatest ever victory. Bannockburn was not the end of the story. The war against English oppression lasted another fourteen years. Bruce lived just long enough to see his dreams of an independent Scotland come to fruition in 1328 with the signing of the Treaty of Edinburgh. The trail takes us to Bruce sites in Scotland, many of the little known and forgotten battle sites in northern England, and as far afield as the Bruce monuments in Andalusia and Jerusalem.

    67 places to visit in Scotland and elsewhere.

    One general map, 3 location maps and a map of Bruce-connected sites in Ireland.

    Bannockburn battle plan.

    Drawings and reproductions of rarely seen illustrations.

*On the Trail of Robert the Bruce* is not all blood and gore. It brings out the love and laughter, pain and passion of one of the great eras of Scottish history. Read it and you will understand why David Ross has never knowingly killed a spider in his life. Once again, he proves himself a master of the popular brand of hands-on history that made *On the Trail of William Wallace* so popular.

'*David R. Ross is a proud patriot and unashamed romantic.*'

SCOTLAND ON SUNDAY

'*Robert the Bruce knew Scotland, knew every class of her people, as no man who ruled her before or since has done. It was he who asked of her a miracle - and she accomplished it.*'

AGNES MUIR MACKENZIE

## On the Trail of Mary Queen of Scots

J. Keith Cheetham

ISBN 0 946487 50 2 PBK £7.99

Life dealt Mary Queen of Scots love, intrigue, betrayal and tragedy in generous measure.

*On the Trail of Mary Queen of Scots* traces the major events in the turbulent life of the beautiful, enigmatic queen whose romantic reign and tragic destiny exerts an undimmed fascination over 400 years after her execution.

    Places of interest to visit – 99 in Scotland, 35 in England and 29 in France.

One general map and 6 location maps.

Line drawings and illustrations.

Simplified family tree of the royal houses of Tudor and Stuart.

Key sites include:

Linlithgow Palace – Mary's birthplace, now a magnificent ruin

Stirling Castle – where, only nine months old, Mary was crowned Queen of Scotland

Notre Dame Cathedral – where, aged fifteen, she married the future king of France

The Palace of Holyroodhouse – Rizzio, one of Mary's closest advisers, was murdered here and some say his blood still stains the spot where he was stabbed to death

Sheffield Castle – where for fourteen years she languished as prisoner of her cousin, Queen Elizabeth I

Fotheringhay – here Mary finally met her death on the executioner's block.

*On the Trail of Mary Queen of Scots* is for everyone interested in the life of perhaps the most romantic figure in Scotland's history; a thorough guide to places connected with Mary, it is also a guide to the complexities of her personal and public life.

'In my end is my beginning'
MARY QUEEN OF SCOTS

'...the woman behaves like the Whore of Babylon'
JOHN KNOX

## On the Trail of Robert Service

GW Lockhart
ISBN 0 946487 24 3 PBK £7.99

Robert Service is famed world-wide for his eye-witness verse-pictures of the Klondike goldrush. As a war poet, his work outsold Owen and Sassoon, and he went on to become the world's first million selling poet. In search of adventure and new experiences, he emigrated from Scotland to Canada in 1890 where he was caught up in the aftermath of the raging gold fever. His vivid dramatic verse bring to life the wild, larger than life characters of the gold rush Yukon, their bar-room brawls, their lust for gold, their trigger-happy gambles with life and love. 'The Shooting of Dan McGrew' is perhaps his most famous poem:

*A bunch of the boys were whooping it up in the*
*Malamute saloon;*
*The kid that handles the music box was hitting a*
*ragtime tune;*
*Back of the bar in a solo game, sat Dangerous*
*Dan McGrew,*
*And watching his luck was his light o'love, the*
*lady that's known as Lou.*

His storytelling powers have brought Robert Service enduring fame, particularly in North America and Scotland where he is something of a cult figure.

Starting in Scotland, *On the Trail of Robert Service* follows Service as he wanders through British Columbia, Oregon, California, Mexico, Cuba, Tahiti, Russia, Turkey and the Balkans, finally 'settling' in France.

This revised edition includes an expanded selection of illustrations of scenes from the Klondike as well as several photographs from the family of Robert Service on his travels around the world.

Wallace Lockhart, an expert on Scottish traditional folk music and dance, is the author of *Highland Balls & Village Halls* and *Fiddles & Folk*. His relish for a well-told tale in popular vernacular led him to fall in love with the verse of Robert Service and write his biography.

'A fitting tribute to a remarkable man - a bank clerk who wanted to become a cowboy. It is hard to imagine a bank clerk writing such lines as:
*A bunch of boys were whooping it up...*
The income from his writing actually exceeded his bank salary by a factor of five and he resigned to pursue a full time writing career.' Charles Munn,
THE SCOTTISH BANKER

'Robert Service claimed he wrote for those who wouldnit be seen dead reading poetry. His was an almost unbelievably mobile life... Lockhart hangs on breathlessly, enthusiastically unearthing clues to the poet's life.' Ruth Thomas,
SCOTTISH BOOK COLLECTOR

'This enthralling biography will delight Service lovers in both the Old World and the New.' Marilyn Wright,
SCOTS INDEPENDENT

## On the Trail of John Muir

Cherry Good
ISBN 0 946487 62 6 PBK £7.99

Follow the man who made the US go green. Confidant of presidents, father of American National Parks, trailblazer of world conservation and voted a Man of the Millennium in the US, John Muir's life and work is of continuing relevance. A man ahead of his time who saw the wilderness he loved threatened by industrialisation and determined to protect it, a crusade in which he was largely successful. His love of the wilderness began at an early age and he was filled with wanderlust all his life.

'Only by going in silence, without baggage, can on truly get into the heart of the wilderness. All other travel is mere dust and hotels and baggage and chatter.' JOHN MUIR

Braving mosquitoes and black bears Cherry Good set herself on his trail – Dunbar, Scotland; Fountain Lake and Hickory Hill, Wisconsin; Yosemite Valley and the Sierra Nevada, California;

the Grand Canyon, Arizona; Alaska; and Canada – to tell his story. John Muir was himself a prolific writer, and Good draws on his books, articles, letters and diaries to produce an account that is lively, intimate, humorous and anecdotal, and that provides refreshing new insights into the hero of world conservation.

John Muir chronology
General map plus 10 detailed maps covering the US, Canada and Scotland
Original colour photographs
Afterword advises on how to get involved
Conservation websites and addresses

Muir's importance has long been acknowledged in the US with over 200 sites of scenic beauty named after him. He was a Founder of The Sierra Club which now has over $^{1}/_{2}$ million members. Due to the movement he started some 360 million acres of wilderness are now protected. This is a book which shows Muir not simply as a hero but as likeable humorous and self-effacing man of extraordinary vision.

*'I do hope that those who read this book will burn with the same enthusiasm for John Muir which the author shows.'*
WEST HIGHLAND FREE PRESS

## On the Trail of Robert Burns

John Cairney
ISBN 0 946487 51 0   PBK   £7.99

Is there anything new to say about Robert Burns?

John Cairney says it's time to trash Burns the Brand and come on the trail of the real Robert Burns. He is the best of travelling companions on this convivial, entertaining journey to the heart of the Burns story.

Internationally known as 'the face of Robert Burns', John Cairney believes that the traditional Burns tourist trail urgently needs to find a new direction. In an acting career spanning forty years he has often lived and breathed Robert Burns on stage. *On the Trail of Robert Burns* shows just how well he can get under the skin of a character. This fascinating journey around Scotland is a rediscovery of Scotland's national bard as a flesh and blood genius.

*On the Trail of Robert Burns* outlines five tours, mainly in Scotland. Key sites include:

Alloway - Burns' birthplace. 'Tam O' Shanter' draws on the witch-stories about Alloway Kirk first heard by Burns in his childhood.
Mossgiel - between 1784 and 1786 in a phenomenal burst of creativity Burns wrote some of his most memorable poems including 'Holy Willie's Prayer' and 'To a Mouse.'
Kilmarnock - the famous Kilmarnock edition of *Poems Chiefly in the Scottish Dialect* published in 1786.
Edinburgh - fame and Clarinda (among others) embraced him.

Dumfries - Burns died at the age of 37. The trail ends at the Burns mausoleum in St Michael's churchyard.

*'For me an aim I never fash*
*I rhyme for fun'.*
ROBERT BURNS

*'My love affair on stage with Burns started in London in 1959. It was consumated on stage at the Traverse Theatre in Edinburgh in 1965 and has continued happily ever since'.*
JOHN CAIRNEY

*'The trail is expertly, touchingly and amusingly followed'.* THE HERALD

## On the Trail of Bonnie Prince Charlie

David R. Ross
ISBN 0 946487 68 5   PBK   £7.99

*On the Trail of Bonnie Prince Charlie* is the story of the Young Pretender. Born in Italy, grandson of James VII, at a time when the German house of Hanover was on the throne, his father was regarded by many as the rightful king. Bonnie Prince Charlie's campaign to retake the throne in his father's name changed the fate of Scotland. The Jacobite movement was responsible for the '45 Uprising, one of the most decisive times in Scottish history. The suffering following the battle of Culloden in 1746 still evokes emotion. Charles' own journey immediately after Culloden is well known: hiding in the heather, escaping to Skye with Flora MacDonald. Little known of is his return to London in 1750 incognito, where he converted to Protestantism (he re-converted to Catholicism before he died and is buried in the Vatican). He was often unwelcome in Europe after the failure of the uprising and came to hate any mention of Scotland and his lost chance.

79 places to visit in Scotland and England
One general map and 4 location maps
Prestonpans, Clifton, Falkirk and Culloden battle plans
Simplified family tree
Rarely seen illustrations

Yet again popular historian David R. Ross brings his own style to one of Scotland's most famous figures. Bonnie Prince Charlie is part of the folklore of Scotland. He brings forth feelings of antagonism from some and romanticism from others, but all agree on his legal right to the throne.

Knowing the story behind the place can bring the landscape to life. Take this book with you on your travels and follow the route taken by Charles' forces on their doomed march.

*'Ross writes with an immediacy, a dynamism, that makes his subjects come alive on the page.'*
DUNDEE COURIER

# NATURAL SCOTLAND

## Wild Scotland: The essential guide to finding the best of natural Scotland

James McCarthy

Photography by Laurie Campbell

ISBN 0 946487 37 5  PBK £7.50

With a foreword by Magnus Magnusson and striking colour photographs by Laurie Campbell, this is the essential up-to-date guide to viewing wildlife in Scotland for the visitor and resident alike. It provides a fascinating overview of the country's plants, animals, bird and marine life against the background of their typical natural settings, as an introduction to the vivid descriptions of the most accessible localities, linked to clear regional maps. A unique feature is the focus on 'green tourism' and sustainable visitor use of the countryside, contributed by Duncan Bryden, manager of the Scottish Tourist Board's Tourism and the Environment Task Force. Important practical information on access and the best times of year for viewing sites makes this an indispensable and user-friendly travelling companion to anyone interested in exploring Scotland's remarkable natural heritage.

James McCarthy is former Deputy Director for Scotland of the Nature Conservancy Council, and now a Board Member of Scottish Natural Heritage and Chairman of the Environmental Youth Work National Development Project Scotland.

## 'Nothing but Heather!'

Gerry Cambridge

ISBN 0 946487 49 9 PBK £15.00

Enter the world of Scottish nature – bizarre, brutal, often beautiful, always fascinating – as seen through the lens and poems of Gerry Cambridge, one of Scotland's most distinctive contemporary poets.

On film and in words, Cambridge brings unusual focus to bear on lives as diverse as those of dragonflies, hermit crabs, short-eared owls, and wood anemones. The result is both an instructive look by a naturalist at some of the flora and fauna of Scotland and a poet's aesthetic journey.

This exceptional collection comprises 48 poems matched with 48 captioned photographs. In his introduction Cambridge explores the origins of the project and the approaches to nature taken by other poets, and incorporates a wry account of an unwillingly-sectarian, farm-labouring, bird-obsessed adolescence in rural Ayrshire in the 1970s.

*'Keats felt that the beauty of a rainbow was somehow tarnished by knowledge of its properties. Yet the natural world is surely made more, not less, marvellous by awareness of its workings. In the poems that accompany these pictures, I have tried to give an inkling of that. May the marriage of verse and image enlarge the reader's appreciation and, perhaps, insight into the chomping, scurrying, quivering, procreating and dying kingdom, however many miles it be beyond the door.'*
GERRY CAMBRIDGE

*'a real poet, with a sense of the music of language and the poetry of life...'* KATHLEEN RAINE
*'one of the most promising and original of modern Scottish poets... a master of form and subtlety.'*
GEORGE MACKAY BROWN

## Scotland Land and People
## An Inhabited Solitude

James McCarthy

ISBN 0 946487 57 X PBK £7.99

*'Scotland is the country above all others that I have seen, in which a man of imagination may carve out his own pleasures; there are so many inhabited solitudes.'* DOROTHY WORDSWORTH, in her journal of August 1803

An informed and thought-provoking profile of Scotland's unique landscapes and the impact of humans on what we see now and in the future. James McCarthy leads us through the many aspects of the land and the people who inhabit it: natural Scotland; the rocks beneath; land ownership; the use of resources; people and place; conserving Scotland's heritage and much more.

Written in a highly readable style, this concise volume offers an under-standing of the land as a whole. Emphasising the uniqueness of the Scottish environment, the author explores the links between this and other aspects of our culture as a key element in rediscovering a modern sense of the Scottish identity and perception of nationhood.

*'This book provides an engaging introduction to the mysteries of Scotland's people and landscapes. Difficult concepts are described in simple terms, providing the interested Scot or tourist with an invaluable overview of the country... It fills an important niche which, to my knowledge, is filled by no other publications.'*

BETSY KING, Chief Executive, Scottish Environmental Education Council.

## The Highland Geology Trail

John L Roberts

ISBN 0946487 36 7  PBK £4.99

Where can you find the oldest rocks in Europe?
Where can you see ancient hills around 800 million years old?
How do you tell whether a valley was carved out by a glacier, not a river?
What are the Fucoid Beds?

Where do you find rocks folded like putty? How did great masses of rock pile up like snow in front of a snow-plough? When did volcanoes spew lava and ash to form Skye, Mull and Rum? Where can you find fossils on Skye?

'...a lucid introduction to the geological record in general, a jargon-free exposition of the regional background, and a series of descriptions of specific localities of geological interest on a 'trail' around the highlands.

Having checked out the local references on the ground, I can vouch for their accuracy and look forward to investigating farther afield, informed by this guide. Great care has been taken to explain specific terms as they occur and, in so doing, John Roberts has created a resource of great value which is eminently usable by anyone with an interest in the outdoors...the best bargain you are likely to get as a geology book in the foreseeable future.'
Jim Johnston, PRESS AND JOURNAL

## Rum: Nature's Island

Magnus Magnusson

ISBN 0 946487 32 4   £7.95 PBK

Rum: Nature's Island is the fascinating story of a Hebridean island from the earliest times through to the Clearances and its period as the sporting playground of a Lancashire industrial magnate, and on to its rebirth as a National Nature Reserve, a model for the active ecological management of Scotland's wild places.

Thoroughly researched and written in a lively accessible style, the book includes comprehensive coverage of the island's geology, animals and plants, and people, with a special chapter on the Edwardian extravaganza of Kinloch Castle. There is practical information for visitors to what was once known as 'the Forbidden Isle'; the book provides details of bothy and other accommodation, walks and nature trails. It closes with a positive vision for the island's future: biologically diverse, economically dynamic and ecologically sustainable.

Rum: Nature's Island is published in co-operation with Scottish Natural Heritage to mark the 40th anniversary of the acquisition of Rum by its predecessor, The Nature Conservancy.

## Red Sky at Night

John Barrington

ISBN 0 946487 60 X   £8.99

'I read John Barrington's book with growing delight. This working shepherd writes beautifully about his animals, about the wildlife, trees and flowers which surround him at all times, and he paints an unforgettable picture of his glorious corner of Western

Scotland. It is a lovely story of a rather wonderful life'.
JAMES HERRIOT

John Barrington is a shepherd to over 750 Blackface ewes who graze 2,000 acres of some of Britain's most beautiful hills overlooking the deep dark water of Loch Katrine in Perthshire. The yearly round of lambing, dipping, shearing and the sales is marvellously interwoven into the story of the glen, of Rob Roy in whose house John now lives, of curling when the ice is thick enough, and of sheep dog trials in the summer. Whether up to the hills or along the glen, John knows the haunts of the local wildlife: the wily hill fox, the grunting badger, the herds of red deer, and the shrews, voles and insects which scurry underfoot. He sets his seasonal clock by the passage of birds on the loch, and jealously guards over the golden eagle's eyrie in the hills. Paul Armstrong's sensitive illustrations are the perfect accompaniment to the evocative text.

'Mr Barrington is a great pleasure to read. One learns more things about the countryside from this account of one year than from a decade of The Archers'.
THE DAILY TELEGRAPH

'Powerful and evocative... a book which brings vividly to life the landscape, the wildlife, the farm animals and the people who inhabit John's vista. He makes it easy for the reader to fall in love with both his surrounds and his commune with nature'.
THE SCOTTISH FIELD

'An excellent and informative book.... not only an account of a shepherd's year but also the diary of a naturalist. Little escapes Barrington's enquiring eye and, besides the life cycle of a sheep, he also gives those of every bird, beast, insect and plant that crosses his path, mixing their histories with descriptions of the geography, local history and folklore of his surroundings'.
TLS

'The family life at Glengyle is wholesome, appealing and not without a touch of the Good Life. Many will envy Mr Barrington his fastness home as they cruise up Loch Katrine on the tourist steamer'.
THE FIELD

## Listen to the Trees

Don MacCaskill

ISBN 0 946487 65 0   £9.99 PBK

Don MacCaskill is one of Scotland's foremost naturalists, conservationists and wildlife photographers. Listen to the Trees is a beautiful and acutely observed account of how his outlook on life began to change as trees, woods, forests and all the wonders that they contain became a focus in his life. It is rich in its portrayal of the life that moves in the Caledonian forest and on the moorlands – lofty twig-stacked heronries, the elusive peregrine falcon and the red, bushy-tailed fox – of the beauty of the trees, and of those who worked in the forests.

'Trees are surely the supreme example of a life-force stronger than our own,' writes Don MacCaskill. 'Some, like the giant redwoods of North America, live for thousands of years. Some, like our own oaks and pines, may live for centuries. All, given the right conditions, will regenerate their species and survive long into the future.'

In the afterword Dr Philip Ratcliffe, former Head of the Forestry Commission's Environment Branch and a leading environment consultant, discusses the future role of Britain's forests – their influence on the natural environment and on the communities that live and work in and around them.

'Listen to the Trees *will inspire all those with an interest in nature. It is a beautiful account, strongly anecdotal and filled with humour.'*
RENNIE McOWAN

*'This man adores trees. 200 years from now, your descendants will know why.'*
JIM GILCHRIST, THE SCOTSMAN

# LUATH GUIDES TO SCOTLAND

These guides are not your traditional where-to-stay and what-to-eat books. They are companions in the rucksack or car seat, providing the discerning traveller with a blend of fiery opinion and moving description. Here you will find *'that curious pastiche of myths and legend and history that the Scots use to describe their heritage... what battle happened in which glen between which clans; where the Picts sacrificed bulls as recently as the 17th century... A lively counterpoint to the more standard, detached guidebook... Intriguing.'*

THE WASHINGTON POST

These are perfect guides for the discerning visitor or resident to keep close by for reading again and again, written by authors who invite you to share their intimate knowledge and love of the areas covered.

## Mull and Iona: Highways and Byways

Peter Macnab

ISBN 0 946487 58 8  PBK  £4.95

'The Isle of Mull is of Isles the fairest,
Of ocean's gems 'tis the first and rarest.'
So a local poet described it a hundred years ago, and this recently revised guide to Mull and sacred Iona, the most accessible islands of the Inner Hebrides, takes the reader on a delightful tour of these rare ocean gems, travelling with a native whose unparalleled knowledge and deep feeling for the area unlock the byways of the islands in all their natural beauty.

## South West Scotland

Tom Atkinson

ISBN 0 946487 04 9  PBK  £4.95

This descriptive guide to the magical country of Robert Burns covers Kyle, Carrick, Galloway, Dumfriesshire, Kirkcudbrightshire and Wigtownshire. Hills, unknown moors and unspoiled beaches grace a land steeped in history and legend and portrayed with affection and deep delight.
An essential book for the visitor who yearns to feel at home in this land of peace and grandeur.

## The West Highlands: The Lonely Lands

Tom Atkinson

ISBN 0 946487 56 1  PBK  £4.95

A guide to Inveraray, Glencoe, Loch Awe, Loch Lomond, Cowal, the Kyles of Bute and all of central Argyll written with insight, sympathy and loving detail. Once Atkinson has taken you there, these lands can never feel lonely. 'I have sought to make the complex simple and the strange familiar,' he writes, and indeed he brings to the land a knowledge and affection only accessible to someone with intimate knowledge of the area.

A must for travellers and natives who want to delve beneath the surface.

*'Highly personal and somewhat quirky... steeped in the lore of Scotland.'*
THE WASHINGTON POST

## The Northern Highlands: The Empty Lands

Tom Atkinson

ISBN 0 946487 55 3  PBK  £4.95

The Highlands of Scotland from Ullapool to Bettyhill and Bonar Bridge to John O' Groats are landscapes of myth and legend, 'empty of people, but of nothing else that brings delight to any tired soul,' writes Atkinson. This highly personal guide describes Highland history and landscape with love, compassion and above all sheer magic.
Essential reading for anyone who has dreamed of the Highlands.

## The North West Highlands: Roads to the Isles

Tom Atkinson

ISBN 0 946487 54 5 PBK £4.95

Ardnamurchan, Morvern, Morar, Moidart and the west coast to Ullapool are included in this guide to the Far West and Far North of Scotland. An unspoiled land of mountains, lochs and silver sands is brought to the walker's toe-tips (and to the reader's fingertips) in this stark, serene and evocative account of town, country and legend.

For any visitor to this Highland wonderland, Queen Victoria's favourite place on earth.

# FOLKLORE

## The Supernatural Highlands

Francis Thompson

ISBN 0 946487 31 6 PBK £8.99

An authoritative exploration of the otherworld of the Highlander, happenings and beings hitherto thought to be outwith the ordinary forces of nature. A simple introduction to the way of life of rural Highland and Island communities, this new edition weaves a path through second sight, the evil eye, witchcraft, ghosts, fairies and other supernatural beings, offering new sight-lines on areas of belief once dismissed as folklore and superstition.

## Scotland: Myth, Legend and Folklore

Stuart McHardy

ISBN: 0 946487 69 3 PBK 7.99

Who were the people who built the megaliths?

What great warriors sleep beneath the Hollow Hills?

Were the early Scottish saints just pagans in disguise?

Was King Arthur really Scottish?

When was Nessie first sighted?

This is a book about Scotland drawn from hundreds, if not thousands of years of story-telling. From the oral traditions of the Scots, Gaelic and Norse speakers of the past, it presents a new picture of who the Scottish are and where they come from. The stories that McHardy recounts may be hilarious, tragic, heroic, frightening or just plain bizzare, but they all provide an insight into a unique tradition of myth, legend and folklore that

has marked both the language and landscape of Scotland.

## Tall Tales from an Island

Peter Macnab

ISBN 0 946487 07 3 PBK £8.99

Peter Macnab was born and reared on Mull. He heard many of these tales as a lad, and others he has listened to in later years.

There are humorous tales, grim tales, witty tales, tales of witchcraft, tales of love, tales of heroism, tales of treachery, historical tales and tales of yesteryear.

A popular lecturer, broadcaster and writer, Peter Macnab is the author of a number of books and articles about Mull, the island he knows so intimately and loves so much. As he himself puts it in his introduction to this book 'I am of the unswerving opinion that nowhere else in the world will you find a better way of life, nor a finer people with whom to share it.'

*'All islands, it seems, have a rich store of characters whose stories represent a kind of sub-culture without which island life would be that much poorer. Macnab has succeeded in giving the retelling of the stories a special Mull flavour, so much so that one can visualise the storytellers sitting on a bench outside the house with a few cronies, puffing on their pipes and listening with nodding approval.'*

WEST HIGHLAND FREE PRESS

## Tales from the North Coast

Alan Temperley

ISBN 0 946487 18 9 PBK £8.99

Seals and shipwrecks, witches and fairies, curses and clearances, fact and fantasy – the authentic tales in this collection come straight from the heart of a small Highland community. Children and adults alike responsd to their timeless appeal. These *Tales of the North Coast* were collected in the early 1970s by Alan Temperley and young people at Farr Secondary School in Sutherland. All the stories were gathered from the area between the Kyle of Tongue and Strath Halladale, in scattered communities wonderfully rich in lore that had been passed on by word of mouth down the generations. This wide-ranging selection provides a satisying balance between intriguing tales of the supernatural and more everyday occurrences. The book also includes chilling eye-witness accounts of the notorious Strathnaver Clearances when tenants were given a few hours to pack up and get out of their homes, which were then burned to the ground.

Underlying the continuity through the generations, this new edition has a foreward by Jim Johnston, the head teacher at Farr, and includes the vigorous linocut images produced by the young people under the guidance of their art teacher, Elliot Rudie.

Since the original publication of this book, Alan Temperley has gone on to become a highly regarded writer for children.

*'The general reader will find this book's spontaneity, its pictures by the children and its fun utterly charming.'* SCOTTISH REVIEW

*'An admirable book which should serve as an encouragement to other districts to gather what remains of their heritage of folk-tales.'*
SCOTTISH EDUCATION JOURNAL

# NEW SCOTLAND

## Scotland - Land and Power the agenda for land reform

Andy Wightman

Foreword by Lesley Riddoch

ISBN 0 946487 70 7 PBK £5.00

What is land reform?

Why is it needed?

Will the Scottish Parliament really make a difference?

*Scotland – Land and Power* argues passionately that nothing less than a radical, comprehensive programme of land reform can make the difference that is needed. Now is no time for palliative solutions which treat the symptoms and not the causes.

*Scotland – Land and Power* is a controversial and provocative book that clarifies the complexities of landownership in Scotland. Andy Wightman explodes the myth that land issues are relevant only to the far flung fringes of rural Scotland, and questions mainstream political commitment to land reform. He presents his own far-reaching programme for change and a pragmatic, inspiring vision of how Scotland can move from outmoded, unjust power structures towards a more equitable landowning democracy.

*'Writers like Andy Wightman are determined to make sure that the hurt of the last century is not compounded by a rushed solution in the next. This accessible, comprehensive but passionately argued book is quite simply essential reading and perfectly timed – here's hoping Scotland's legislators agree.'*
LESLEY RIDDOCH

## Old Scotland New Scotland

Jeff Fallow

ISBN 0 946487 40 5 PBK £6.99

'Together we can build a new Scotland based on Labour's values.' DONALD DEWAR, Party Political Broad-cast

'Despite the efforts of decent Mr Dewar, the voters may yet conclude they are looking at the same old

hacks in brand new suits.' IAN BELL, *The Independent*

'At times like this you suddenly realise how dangerous the neglect of Scottish history in our schools and universities may turn out to be.' MICHAEL FRY, *The Herald*

'...one of the things I hope will go is our chip on the shoulder about the English... The SNP has a huge responsibility to articulate Scottish independence in a way that is pro-Scottish and not anti-English.' ALEX SALMOND, *The Scotsman*

Scottish politics have never been more exciting. In *old Scotland new Scotland* Jeff Fallow takes us on a graphic voyage through Scotland's turbulent history, from earliest times through to the present day and beyond. This fast-track guide is the quick way to learn what your history teacher didn't tell you, essential reading for all who seek an understanding of Scotland and its history.

Eschewing the romanticisation of his country's past, Fallow offers a new perspective on an old nation. *'Too many people associate Scottish history with tartan trivia or outworn romantic myth. This book aims to blast that stubborn idea.'* JEFF FALLOW

## Notes from the North incorporating a Brief History of the Scots and the English

Emma Wood

ISBN 0 946487 46 4 PBK £8.99

Notes on being English
Notes on being in Scotland
Learning from a shared past

Sickened by the English jingoism that surfaced in rampant form during the 1982 Falklands War, Emma Wood started to dream of moving from her home in East Anglia to the Highlands of Scotland. She felt increasingly frustrated and marginalised as Thatcherism got a grip on the southern English psyche. The Scots she met on frequent holidays in the Highlands had no truck with Thatcherism, and she felt at home with grass-roots Scottish anti-authoritarianism. The decision was made. She uprooted and headed for a new life in the north of Scotland.

*'An intelligent and perceptive book... calm, reflective, witty and sensitive. It should certainly be read by all English visitors to Scotland, be they tourists or incomers. And it should certainly be read by all Scots concerned about what kind of nation we live in. They might learn something about themselves.'* THE HERALD

*'... her enlightenment is evident on every page of this perceptive, provocative book.'*
MAIL ON SUNDAY

# FICTION

## The Bannockburn Years

William Scott

ISBN 0 946487 34 0  PBK  £7.95

A present day Edinburgh solicitor stumbles across reference to a document of value to the Nation State of Scotland. He tracks down the document on the Isle of Bute, a document which probes the real 'quaestiones' about nationhood and national identity. The document ends up being published, but is it authentic and does it matter? Almost 700 years on, these 'quaestiones' are still worth asking.

Written with pace and passion, William Scott has devised an intriguing vehicle to open up new ways of looking at the future of Scotland and its people. He presents an alternative interpretation of how the Battle of Bannockburn was fought, and through the Bannatyne manuscript he draws the reader into the minds of those involved.

Winner of the 1997 Constable Trophy, the premier award in Scotland for an unpublished novel, this book offers new insights to both the academic and the general reader which are sure to provoke further discussion and debate.

*'A brilliant storyteller. I shall expect to see your name writ large hereafter.'*

NIGEL TRANTER, October 1997.

*'... a compulsive read.'* PH Scott, THE SCOTSMAN

## The Great Melnikov

Hugh Maclachlan

ISBN 0 946487 42 1  PBK  £7.95

A well crafted, gripping novel, written in a style reminiscent of John Buchan and set in London and the Scottish Highlands during the First World War, *The Great Melnikov* is a dark tale of double-cross and deception. We first meet Melnikov, one-time star of the German circus, languishing as a down-and-out in Trafalgar Square. He soon finds himself drawn into a tortuous web of intrigue. He is a complex man whose personal struggle with alcoholism is an inner drama which parallels the tense twists and turns as a spy mystery unfolds. Melnikov's options are narrowing. The circle of threat is closing. Will Melnikov outwit the sinister enemy spy network? Can he summon the will and the wit to survive?

Hugh Maclachlan, in his first full length novel, demonstrates an undoubted ability to tell a good story well. His earlier stories have been broadcast on Radio Scotland, and he has the rare distinction of being shortlisted for the Macallan/Scotland on Sunday Short Story Competition two years in succession.

*'... a satisfying rip-roarer of a thriller... an undeniable*

*page turner, racing along to a suitably cinematic ending, richly descriptive yet clear and lean.'*

THE SCOTSMAN

## Grave Robbers

Robin Mitchell

ISBN 0 946487 72 3  PBK  £7.95

After years of sleeping peacefully, the deceased dignitaries of Old Edinburgh are about to get a nasty surprise...

Grave-digger and funeral enthusiast Cameron Carter lives a relatively quiet life. Until a misplaced shovel cracks open a coffin lid and reveals a hidden fortune, that is. Nearly one hundred and seventy years after the trial of Scotland's notorious body snatchers, William Burke and William Hare, the ancient trade of grave robbing returns to the town's cemeteries.

Forming an unholy union with small time crook, Adam, Cameron is drawn into a web of crime that involves a bogus American Scholars' Society, chocolate chip ice cream and Steve McQueen. Their sacrilegious scheming doesn't go quite to plan, however, and events begin to spiral dangerously beyond Cameron the answers will be exhumed.

Will our hero pull the tour guide of his dreams?

Will his partner in crime ever shift those microwaves?

Is there an afterlife?

In Robin Mitchell's rude and darkly comic debut novel, all the answers will be exhumed.

*'Good, unclean macabre fun from Robin Mitchell...'*

IAN RANKIN

## But n Ben A-Go-Go

Matthew Fitt

ISBN 0 946487 82 0  HBK  £10.99

The year is 2090. Global flooding has left most of Scotland under water. The descendants of those who survived God's Flood live in a community of floating island parishes, known collectively as Port.

Port's citizens live in mortal fear of Senga, a supervirus whose victims are kept in a giant hospital warehouse in sealed capsules called Kists.

Paolo Broon is a low-ranking cyberjanny. His life-partner, Nadia, lies forgotten and alone in Omega Kist 624 in the Rigo Imbeki Medical Center. When he receives an unexpected message  from his radge criminal father to meet him at But n Ben A-Go-Go, Paolo's life is changed forever.

He must traverse VINE, Port and the Drylands and deal with rebel American tourists and crabbit Dundonian microchips to discover the truth about his family's past in order to free Nadia from the sair grip of the merciless Senga.

Set in a distinctly unbonnie future-Scotland, the

novel's dangerous atmosphere and psychologically-malkied characters weave a tale that both chills and intrigues. In *But n Ben A-Go-Go* Matthew Fitt takes the allegedly dead language of Scots and energises it with a narrative that crackles and fizzes with life.

*'After an initial shock, readers of this sprightly and imaginative tale will begin to relish its verbal impetus, where a standard Lallans, laced with bits of Dundonian and Aberdonian, is stretched and skelped to meet the demands of cyberjannies and virtual hoorhooses.*

*Eurobawbees, rooburgers, mutant kelpies, and titanic blooters from supertyphoons make sure that the Scottish peninsula is no more parochial than its language. I recommend an entertaining and groundbreaking book.'*
EDWIN MORGAN

*'Matthew Fitt's instinctive use of Scots is spellbinding. This is an assured novel of real inventiveness. Be prepared to boldly go...'*
ELLIE McDONALD

*'Easier to read than Shakespeare – wice the fun.'*
DES DILLON

# HISTORY

## Blind Harry's Wallace
William Hamilton of Gilbertfield

Introduced by Elspeth King

ISBN 0 946487 43 X  HBK  £15.00
ISBN 0 946487 33 2  PBK  £8.99

The original story of the real braveheart, Sir William Wallace. Racy, blood on every page, violently anglophobic, grossly embellished, vulgar and disgusting, clumsy and stilted, a literary failure, a great epic.

Whatever the verdict on BLIND HARRY, this is the book which has done more than any other to frame the notion of Scotland's national identity. Despite its numerous 'historical inaccuracies', it remains the principal source for what we now know about the life of Wallace.

The novel and film *Braveheart* were based on the 1722 Hamilton edition of this epic poem. Burns, Wordsworth, Byron and others were greatly influenced by this version 'wherein the old obsolete words are rendered more intelligible', which is said to be the book, next to the Bible, most commonly found in Scottish households in the eighteenth century. Burns even admits to having 'borrowed... a couplet worthy of Homer' directly from Hamilton's version of BLIND HARRY to include in 'Scots wha hae'.

Elspeth King, in her introduction to this, the first accessible edition of BLIND HARRY in verse form since 1859, draws parallels between the situation in Scotland at the time of Wallace and that in Bosnia and Chechnya in the 1990s. Seven hundred years to the day after the Battle of Stirling Bridge, the 'Settled Will of the Scottish People' was expressed in the devolution referendum of 11 September 1997.

She describes this as a landmark opportunity for mature reflection on how the nation has been shaped, and sees BLIND HARRY'S WALLACE as an essential and compelling text for this purpose.

*'A true bard of the people'.*
TOM SCOTT, THE PENGUIN BOOK OF SCOTTISH VERSE, on Blind Harry.

*'A more inventive writer than Shakespeare'.*
RANDALL WALLACE

*'The story of Wallace poured a Scottish prejudice in my veins which will boil along until the floodgates of life shut in eternal rest'.* ROBERT BURNS

*'Hamilton's couplets are not the best poetry you will ever read, but they rattle along at a fair pace. In reissuing this work, the publishers have re-opened the spring from which most of our conceptions of the Wallace legend come'.*
SCOTLAND ON SUNDAY

*'The return of Blind Harry's Wallace, a man who makes Mel look like a wimp'.* THE SCOTSMAN

## Reportage Scotland: History in the Making
Louise Yeoman

Foreword by Professor David Stevenson

ISBN 0 946487 61 8  PBK  £9.99

Events – both major and minor – as seen and recorded by Scots throughout history.

Which king was murdered in a sewer?
What was Dr Fian's love magic?
Who was the half-roasted abbot?
Which cardinal was salted and put in a barrel?
Why did Lord Kitchener's niece try to blow up Burns's cottage?

The answers can all be found in this eclectic mix covering nearly 2000 years of Scottish history. Historian Louise Yeoman's rummage through the manuscript, book and newspaper archives of the National Library of Scotland has yielded an astonishing range of material from a letter to the king of the Picts to in Mary Queen of Scots' own account of the murder of David Riccio; from the execution of William Wallace to accounts of anti-poll tax actions and the opening of the new Scottish Parliament. The book takes pieces from the original French, Latin, Gaelic and Scots and makes them accessible to the general reader, often for the first time.

The result is compelling reading for anyone interested in the history that has made Scotland what it is today.

*'Marvellously illuminating and wonderfully readable'.*
Angus Calder, SCOTLAND ON SUNDAY

*'A monumental achievement in drawing together such a rich historical harvest'*
Chris Holme, THE HERALD

# SOCIAL HISTORY

## A Word for Scotland

Jack Campbell

with a foreword by Magnus Magnusson

ISBN 0 946487 48 0 PBK £12.99

'A word for Scotland' was Lord Beaver-brook's hope when he founded the *Scottish Daily Express*. That word for Scotland quickly became, and was for many years, the national newspaper of Scotland.

The pages of *A Word For Scotland* exude warmth and a wry sense of humour. Jack Campbell takes us behind the scenes to meet the larger-than-life characters and ordinary people who made and recorded the stories. Here we hear the stories behind the stories that hit the headlines in this great yarn of journalism in action.

It would be true to say 'all life is here'. From the Cheapside Street fire of which cost the lives of 19 Glasgow firemen, to the theft of the Stone of Destiny, to the lurid exploits of serial killer Peter Manuel, to encounters with world boxing champions Benny Lynch and Cassius Clay - this book offers telling glimpses of the characters, events, joy and tragedy which make up Scotland's story in the 20th century.

*'As a rookie reporter you were proud to work on it and proud to be part of it - it was fine newspaper right at the heartbeat of Scotland.'*

RONALD NEIL, Chief Executive of BBC Production, and a reporter on the *Scottish Daily Express* (1963-68)

*'This book is a fascinating reminder of Scottish journalism in its heyday. It will be read avidly by those journalists who take pride in their profession – and should be compulsory reading for those who don't.'*

JACK WEBSTER, columnist on *The Herald* and *Scottish Daily Express* journalist (1960-80)

## The Crofting Years

Francis Thompson

ISBN 0 946487 06 5 PBK £6.95

Crofting is much more than a way of life. It is a storehouse of cultural, linguistic and moral values which holds together a scattered and struggling rural population. This book fills a blank in the written history of crofting over the last two centuries. Bloody conflicts and gunboat diplomacy, treachery, compassion, music and story: all figure in this mine of information on crofting in the Highlands and Islands of Scotland.

*'I would recommend this book to all who are interested in the past, but even more so to those who are interested in the future survival of our way of life and culture'*

STORNOWAY GAZETTE

*'The book is a mine of information on many aspects of the past, among them the homes, the food, the music and the medicine of our crofting forebears.'*

John M Macmillan, erstwhile CROFTERS COMMISSIONER FOR LEWIS AND HARRIS

## Shale Voices

Alistair Findlay

foreword by Tam Dalyell MP

ISBN 0 946487 63 4 PBK £10.99

ISBN 0 946487 78 2 HBK £17.99

*'He was at Addiewell oil works. Anyone goes in there is there for keeps.'* JOE, Electrician

*'There's shale from here to Ayr, you see.'* DICK, a Drawer

*'The way I describe it is, you're a coal miner and I'm a shale miner. You're a tramp and I'm a toff.'* HARRY, a Drawer

*'There were sixteen or eighteen Simpsons... ...She was having one every dividend we would say.'* SISTERS, from Broxburn

*Shale Voices* offers a fascinating insight into shale mining, an industry that employed generations of Scots, had an impact on the social, political and cultural history of Scotland and gave birth to today's large oil companies. Author Alistair Findlay was born in the shale mining village of Winchburgh and is the fourth son of a shale miner, Bob Findlay, who became editor of the *West Lothian Courier*. *Shale Voices* combines oral history, local journalism and family history. The generations of communities involved in shale mining provide, in their own words, a unique documentation of the industry and its cultural and political impact.

Photographs, drawings, poetry and short stories make this a thought provoking and entertaining account. It is as much a joy to dip into and feast the eyes on as to read from cover to cover.

*'Alistair Findlay has added a basic source material to the study of Scottish history that is invaluable and will be of great benefit to future generations. Scotland owes him a debt of gratitude for undertaking this work.'* TAM DALYELL MP

# TRAVEL & LEISURE

## Edinburgh and Leith Pub Guide

Stuart McHardy

ISBN 0 946487 80 4 PBK £4.95

You might be in Edinburgh to explore the closes and wynds of one of Europe's most beautiful cities, to sample the finest Scotch whiskies and to discover a rich Celtic heritage of traditional music and story-telling. Or you might be in Leith to get trashed. Either way, this is the guide for you.

With the able assistance of his long time drinking partner, 'the Man from Fife', Stuart McHardy has dragged his tired old frame around over two hundred pubs – all in the name of research, of course. Alongside drinking numerous pints, he has managed to compile enough historical anecdote and practical information to allow anyone with a sturdy liver to follow in his footsteps.

Although Stuart unashamedly gives top marks to his favourite haunts, he rates most highly those pubs that are original, distinctive and cater to the needs of their clientele. Be it domino league or play-station league, pina colada or a pint of heavy, filled foccacia or mince and tatties, Stuart has found a decent pub that does it.

Over 200 pubs

12 pub trails plus maps

Helpful rating system

Brief guide to Scottish beers and whiskies

'The Man from Fife's wry take on each pub

Discover the answers to such essential questions as:

Which pubs are recommended by whisky wholesalers for sampling?

Where can you find a pub that has links with Bonnie Prince Charlie and Mary Queen of Scots?

Which pub serves kangaroo burgers?

Where can you go for a drop of mead in Edinburgh?

Which pub has a toy crocodile in pride of place behind the bar?

How has Stuart survived all these years?

Long familiar with Edinburgh and Leith's drinking dens, watering holes, shebeens and dens of iniquity, Stuart McHardy has penned a bible for the booze connoisseur. Whether you're here for Hogmanay, a Six Nations weekend, the Festival, just one evening or the rest of your life, this is the companion to slip in your pocket or handbag as you venture out in search of the craic.

## Edinburgh's Historic Mile

Duncan Priddle

ISBN 0 946487 97 9  PBK £2.99

This ancient thoroughfare runs downwards and eastwards for just over a mile. Its narrow closes and wynds, each with a distinctive atmosphere and character, have their own stories to tell. From the looming fortress of the Castle at the top, to the Renaissance beauty of the palace at the bottom, every step along this ancient highway brings the city's past to life – a past both glorious and gory.

Written with all the knowledge and experience the Witchery Tours have gathered in 15 years, it is full of quirky, fun and fascinating stories that you wont find anywhere else.

Designed to fit easily in pocket or bag and with a comprehensive map on the back cover this is the perfect book to take on a walk in Edinburgh or read before you arrive.

## Pilgrims In The Rough:
## St Andrews beyond the 19th hole

Michael Tobert

ISBN 0 946487 74 X  PBK £7.99

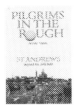

'A travel book about St. Andrews. A book that combines the game I love and the course I have played for 20 years, with the town that I consider as close to paradise as I am likely to find on this side of the pearly gates.'
MICHAEL TOBERT

With ghosts, witches and squabbling clerics, *Pilgrims in the Rough* is a funny and affectionate portrayal of Michael Tobert's home town. The author has always wanted to write a travel book – but he has done more than that. Combining tourist information with history, humour and anecdote, he has written a book that will appeal to golfer and non golfer, local and visitor, alike.

While *Pilgrims in the Rough* is more than just a guide to clubs and caddies, it is nonetheless packed with information for the golf enthusiast. It features a detailed map of the course and the low down from a regular St Andrews player on booking times, the clubs and each of the holes on the notorious Old Course.

The book also contains an informative guide to the attractions of the town and the best places to stay and to eat out. Michael Tobert's infectious enthusiasm for St Andrews will even persuade the most jaded golf widow or widower that the town is worth a visit!

'An extraordinary book' THE OBSERVER

'Tobert displays genuine erudition on such topics as the history of the cathedral and university and, of course, the tricky business of playing the Old Course itself.' THE SCOTSMAN

# POETRY
## Poems to be read aloud

Collected and with an introduction by Tom Atkinson

ISBN 0 946487 00 6  PBK £5.00

This personal collection of doggerel and verse ranging from the tear-jerking *Green Eye of the Yellow God* to the rarely printed, bawdy *Eskimo Nell* has a lively cult following. Much borrowed and rarely returned, this is a book for reading aloud in very good company, preferably after a dram or twa. You are guaranteed a warm welcome if you arrive at a gathering with this little volume in your pocket.

## **Luath** Press Limited
*committed to publishing well written books worth reading*

LUATH PRESS takes its name from Robert Burns, whose little collie Luath (*Gael.,* swift or nimble) tripped up Jean Armour at a wedding and gave him the chance to speak to the woman who was to be his wife and the abiding love of his life. Burns called one of *The Twa Dogs* Luath after Cuchullin's hunting dog in *Ossian's Fingal*. Luath Press grew up in the heart of Burns country, and now resides a few steps up the road from Burns' first lodgings in Edinburgh's Royal Mile.

Luath offers you distinctive writing with a hint of unexpected pleasures.

Most UK and US bookshops either carry our books in stock or can order them for you. To order direct from us, please send a £sterling cheque, postal order, international money order or your credit card details (number, address of cardholder and expiry date) to us at the address below. Please add post and packing as follows: UK – £1.00 per delivery address; overseas surface mail – £2.50 per delivery address; overseas airmail – £3.50 for the first book to each delivery address, plus £1.00 for each additional book by airmail to the same address. If your order is a gift, we will happily enclose your card or message at no extra charge.

**Luath** Press Limited
543/2 Castlehill
The Royal Mile
Edinburgh EH1 2ND
Scotland
Telephone: 0131 225 4326 (24 hours)
Fax: 0131 225 4324
email: gavin.macdougall@luath.co.uk
Website: www.luath.co.uk